Y0-DNJ-361

Love
SISY
DeeDeeDeen

CODE RED

A SILVERSTONE BAY STORY

Copyright © 2013 DeeDeeDeen. The Book author
retains sole copyright to his or her contributions to
this book.

ISBN: 13-978-0-9837049-6-6
ISBN-10:0-983704961

Table of Content

Prologue

You will recall from Code Black-A Silverstone Bay Story, Lolena Wynn and Hercules McMarshall had kissed, a long passionate kiss, for the very first time in front of everyone at Silverstone Bay High School Football Stadium. This kiss had been brewing for a long time, a very long time! It was a kiss that Lolena wanted to give to Hercules, over twenty years ago, to show her sincere appreciation for bringing an end to the torment the female soldiers were subject to at the hands of a few evil male soldiers who had raped, with no regards to the feelings, dignity or mere human rights of their victims. However, Lolena was not going to and did not live her life as a victim. Look at her at this moment; the crowd just unanimously, elected her to be the write-in candidate for the newly vacated mayor position. Everyone was looking at her and Hercules embraced in a kiss the whole world saw, but only Lolena and Hercules were in that world at that moment. Lolena released her hurt, pain, and fear, along with her joy, dreams and years of pinned up passion. For Lolena, it had been quite some time since she'd been kissed.

Hercules held Lolena firmly but ever so gently. He was holding his jewel in his arms. He was kissing the woman of his dreams with the vigor of a lion, and he did not care who was watching. The world was watching. The world was on his side. They all saw how much he loved Lolena Wynn. When he first saw her, dancing in the sexy red dress, he knew right then that this is the love of his life. She is the woman he searched for his entire life. He kissed her with all of his might.

You remember Smokey Mike, he had come up to the happy couple; and politely interrupted the passionate pair and brought them back to the moment, "Hey Herc, "We're on our way to Dominic's. Are we going to see you there?" Smokey was the owner and operator of Dominic's; the place where you were there, only if you were suppose to be there.

You remember Sonnie, the brotha who's bringing back the fedora, he had walked up and announced, "Well, it's been fun but I'm about to go have some real fun!" Hercules asked him, "You and the Mrs. have a date?" Sonnie smiled and slickly said, "I have a date alright." What did Sonnie mean when he said that?

You remember Rafeki, the brotha who has an opinion about everything and most times, his opinions are right. He joined the group, but he was still in Ready mode; he was observing all the activity that was going on at the stadium. The stadium had been in an uproar just moments earlier. While the audience was watching a video tribute for Mr. Michaels, the high-school teacher murdered in the driveway of his house, a 'Caught-On-Tape' video interrupted that video. The video showed the mayor and the chief of police at the Solo Political Debate when they did not know the local news crew was recording their conversation and the conversation divulged the crooked details of the plot to takeover Silverstone Bay. Everyone at the stadium heard and watched, with pure shock and rage, that the two city officials were behind all of the criminal activity, and they were a part of the kidnapping of Kayla Spencer who miraculously was returned to her parents tonight at the stadium. Rafeki looked towards the announcer's booth and said Hercules, "Do you see that camera?"

You remember Nathaniel, the brotha who loves to ride horses and wears his cowboy hat all the time, he and his wife walked up to the group. He proudly acknowledged to the group, "Looks like we were ready!" and the Brothas all proudly brotha dap...and Nathaniel and his family went home to rest up for the rodeo the next day. "Hope to see my Brothas there!" were his departing words.

Sherwood, Hercules' brotha from another mother, walked up with his wife and children, and he embraced all his brothas, but he laughingly whispered into Hercules' ear, "I don't think it's goin' to be hangin' low tonight." Hercules laughed at their inside joke and cut his eyes at his partner and gave him a sly grin.

The camera Rafeki spotted was actively recording. The secret group was watching and observing all the activity at the stadium. Silverstone Bay, the jewel by the Sea, became a target of the secret group. Bernard Ellington had his eye on Silverstone Bay when he saw Hercules McMarshall on a TV interview. He had recognized him from college. If you had to blame anyone for the troubles Silverstone Bay experienced, you could point your finger directly at Mr. Bernard Ellington. He lived his life blaming everyone else for his shortcomings. In reality, his shortcomings were all conjured up in his own head. He was the cause of his own issues. He felt all of his problems started when he was in college, and he wanted to play football because he wanted to be close to his father. His father was the coach of the college football team. Bernard wasn't a very good player but his father reluctantly let him play during the last play of the championship game, and all Bernard had to do was throw the ball to the black guy, 'the Code Black play'. The mistake happened because the coach took Hercules out of the game and put in Bernard and they didn't know whom to throw the ball to! The team lost, everyone was disappointed and that changed Bernard for the worst; he hatched his 'Code Black' plan when years later he saw that interview of Hercules. He still blamed Hercules for all his troubles. Bernard can be a very convincing man. He was successful in manipulating a certain kind of person. He manipulated people like the mayor, the chief of police, Mr. Green, Mr. Jason and Ball Player. He thought he had Philip, his butler, under control, but he found out, Philip had him under control. However, his empire has not entirely crumbled. Who's the lady with the accented voice spewing the words, "Code Black is now Code Red...?"

CODE RED

A SILVERSTONE BAY STORY

Your Husband Didn't Make It

"Your husband is dead," moaned Ernest Green as he continued to sex Jennifer Jason harder and harder. Ernest's body was radiating so much heat you could see the steam come off him, and a fountain of sweat dripped onto the bubbly bosoms of his favorite sex partner. He and Jennifer Jason had been sex partners for several years. Yes, she married his long-time business partner, Keith Jason, who now is his dead business partner, but Ernest, who preferred Mr. G, broke the news to his now widowed wife.

Mr. G, remarkably well endowed, enjoyed pleasuring Jennifer; she was an animal in bed. She knew exactly how to satisfy his insatiable sexual appetite for her plump, juicy VA JJ. He was pumping her real hard right at that moment; he pumped in and out, in and out, fast than slow, fast than slow. He would slow his motion down and pull his Johnson out to the tip and tease her a little with smooth, baby strokes and then push it all the way in, grinding her pelvis harder and harder. She bucked with ecstasy repeatedly. Before she calmed down, Mr. G flipped her over and he started licking and sucking the back of her neck and ears. He kissed and licked her shoulders. He massaged her back, grabbed her juicy behind and kissed it. Then he entered her from behind. He was slow to start. He watched her cry out with pleasure. She was panting quickly and muttering inaudible words, "mo, mo, more, ha, ha, harder, do, do, do it." Mr. G. started pumping hard and fast. His Johnson was wet, slippery and hard. "Ummm, Ummm, yeah, you like it when I ram that pretty ass of yours, here, take it, take it. My load is coming, get ready for it. Grrrrrrr," oozed out of his mouth. He continued to rock her from behind for many moments more. She was screaming now. It was loud and strong. She grabbed the pillow and started biting it to control her sounds. Then he came. Mr. G pulled his Johnson out and unloaded his load all over her back. He used his hand to jerk the last of his load onto her. She turned over and looked up at him; her eyes went down to his semi-erect cock, and she sat up and started sucking it. She took him in her hand and stroked then licked, then sucked. Mr. G watched her, and he got hard again. She continued to suck and then he unloaded in her mouth, "take it, take it, yeah, take it."

They continued to lie in the large, ski-sled styled bed which sat two extra feet off the floor and covered with 1500-count, gold, silk bed sheets and a beautiful, multiple-covered quilt. The fire flames that burned in the fireplace danced on the wood-paneled wall decorated with beautiful artwork from Spain added to the cozy ambiance in the cabin nested in the woods of Camp Bridge, Wyoming. This beautiful hide-away cabin reserved regularly for the sexual escapades of this deceiving couple even though they would have sex anywhere they chose to have sex. They did not limit this activity to just this bedroom. They were so daring at times they would sneak away to get a quickie wherever they found a spot. There were many times they had sex with people in the next room. Since Jennifer's husband regularly worked closely with Mr. G, they would grab a quickie in a bathroom, or a closet, or the back seat of the car or down in the basement, or the garage or any place they could find that would allow them to screw each other's brains out. Mr. G and Jennifer did not love each other; they did not like each other; they just used each other for sex. They created a truly sick relationship. Mr. G would have sex with Jennifer, then go back into the room, and resume the meeting with her husband.

The last assignment that Mr. G and Keith Jason had was to takeover Silverstone Bay via Code Black, the diabolical plot conjured up by, leader, Mr. Bernard Ellington, to infiltrate Silverstone Bay through the cooperative help of the city's mayor and chief of police. They enlisted the criminal services of a local street rat by the name Ball Player. They were going to move into town by, first, running out a good portion of the citizens. They did that by creating a two-year crime wave; no activity was off the table. There were murders, robberies, forced business closures, kidnappings, forced house foreclosures, and cash offering for properties. They mainly wanted to take over the old military base and convert it to a private prison industrial complex. They were looking forward to receiving payment for all the inmates sentenced there.

An added bonus was the location of the city and the weather. Silverstone Bay, California located in northern California about 20 miles south of San Francisco. Ten miles of the city are ocean front properties, and at the end of the oceanfront, the land begins to go up to hillside views of the ocean. Then it goes further up to higher hills, mountains and forest views and turns inward. The entire city is twenty miles long and twenty miles wide. Some homes sat nested in the hills, many homes spread for miles on the low lands. The weather was tropical all year round. The tropical weather was the main reason Jennifer wanted Silverstone Bay. The cold weather bored her. She had just told her husband that a few months ago. They went to a meeting at Mr. Ellington's house; he lived on the other side of Camp Bridge. The town was not densely populated; the citizens lived sporadically throughout the woods. They had a meeting to discuss the last few details of the Code Black plan. A few weeks after that meeting, the secret group relocated to Silverstone Bay to put the final steps in motion for the big takeover.

Jennifer Jason was a scorned bitch. She came to America from Spain when she was nineteen. She spoke fluent English with a strong, sexy accent. Her voice was so sensuous you tasted the sex in her words as she spoke. She is a cunningly smart woman, and her natural beauty is what woman paid thousands of dollars to replicate. She did not take no for an answer, and no man turned her down; well no man except Hercules McMarshall.

When she came to America, she first went to college in Arizona. She attended college when Hercules attended. Hercules was popular, handsome, and the best football player the college had on their team. Jennifer made a play for Hercules, but he had no interest in her. She never forgot that rejection. A few years later, she ran into Mr. Ellington. Through the course of that conversation, they realized they attended college during the same period and discovered they shared the same discontent for Hercules McMarshall. Mr. Ellington introduced her to Keith Jason. She liked his dimples. She married him the next weekend. She thanked Mr. Ellington for the introduction one drunken night.

Keith Jason fell in love with Jennifer the first time he saw her. Keith was a handsome man; he had a perfect set of pearly whites and deep-set dimples that made women cream. He used it to his advantage whenever possible. He used it when he first met Jennifer; he smiled at her, and it worked like clockwork, however, this sensual magic over women was all he had. He chose the fast life style; the quicker he could get what he wanted, he took that route; his friendship with Mr. Ellington benefitted him because all he did was use his muscle to accomplish whatever dastardly deed Mr. Ellington conjured up. Keith Jason was, basically, stupid smart.

Jennifer Jason had her husband wrapped around her evil fingers. Upon receiving the news that her husband was dead while she was in the act of having rough sex with his close business partner was not enough to disturb her, upset her, shock her or even stop her from continuing the sexual activity. No, not she, to her it was just the cost of doing business.

"I thought that would happen," Jennifer said as she stared at the fire burning in the fireplace. "When

7

did you find out?" She asked. "Shortly after we finished watching the video feed this evening. The drop did not go the way we planned. That crew that Ball Player character hired, taken out; your husband shot in the head, Ellington and Ball Player taken into custody. The Code Black safe house location captured," he answered.

Earlier that evening, Jennifer watched intently the video feed from Silverstone Bay High School where she would witness the finale of the Code Black plan. Instead of viewing the assassination of Lolena Wynn and then the random assassinations of several of the innocent people attending the event, Jennifer watched her dream deteriorate right in front of her eyes. At that moment, the Code Red plan became effective. "Code Black is now Code Red," she said seductively.

Let's Just Celebrate

Lolena Wynn stood on the erected stage on the football field at Silverstone Bay High School. Hercules McMarshall stood next to her. They watched the crowd begin to depart. The extraordinary events that took place that evening caused the postponement of the varsity football game.

Silverstone Bay will never be the same again. Tonight, prayers answered, criminals captured and defeated, diabolical forces exposed, and now, the city, the Jewel by the Sea could begin to lick its wounds. There was so much to be thankful, but the abundance of thankfulness manifested would not be enough to bring back all the loved ones or ease the pain of those victimized by the so-called Code Black plan. History repeated itself in Silverstone Bay; the destructive history of systematic forces victimizing innocent people for selfish gains.

It took a while for people to begin to leave the stadium. The audience witnessed how their own mayor and chief of police allowed and participated in the systematic destruction of their fair city. Some people were so upset they cried, screamed, and yelled. It brought several people to their knees in disbelief. The authorities quickly hustled Mayor Burton and Chief Jennings away after the audience witnessed the details of the plot to destroy the city, by any means necessary, on the video screen.

The city was blessed this evening when Kayla Spencer miraculously returned to her parents after being missing for two years. On her way home from school, Mr. Ellington kidnapped and held her captive. It was a gift from heaven when she ran to the arms of her elated parents. The Spencers did not give up hope on seeing their daughter again. It was hard on them; it took its toll mentally, physically and spiritually, but now they can begin to heal. Everyone around them hugged, cried and rejoiced. The

10

Spencers had to be escorted out quickly; it was extremely overwhelming for the family. Time will tell on how well Kayla survived the ordeal.

Hercules embraced Lolena and asked, "How are you? How are you doing this moment in time? Your world has changed in just a matter of minutes, but before you answer, I want to say, I love you, Lolena, and for a moment there, I thought I almost lost you." Lolena looked at Hercules, and she saw tears in his eyes. "Hercules, sweetheart, you're my hero. You don't have to worry about ever losing me," she spoke to him with tears in her voice. They kissed each other again. "Before anything else happens, let's just go celebrate," Hercules suggested. "I am right there with you, baby. Let's go," Lolena agreed.

Hercules and Lolena were on their way to the parking lot; Sixty B Mackin came up behind them and grabbed his mother from behind. "Hey mom, are you okay? Things got wild up in this mother fuc... I mean this place, tonight! Did you see that?! They took that bitch ass, I mean that donkey's behind mayor and fake ass, I mean, fake donkey's behind Five O outta here in handcuffs! Now, that's what I'm talking about! And, Little Princess returned home.

11

Wow, things could not have been better! Where you two love birds going? After that kiss which the whole world saw, y'all gonna get a room?" He teased. Lolena was so glad to see her son; she hugged and kissed him on the cheek. "Oh wait a minute, it did get better; the city folk want you to be mayor! Mom, you mayor of Silverstone Bay; what will that make me, the first son? Hey, that sounds real cool, Sixty B Mackin, first son of Silverstone Bay."

After the authorities carted off the corrupt city officials, the people at the stadium unanimously elected Lolena to be the write-in candidate for the newly open mayor position. She can still hear the crowd, "Lolena Wynn, write her in. Lolena Wynn, write her in. Lolena Wynn, write her in." Lolena hadn't had any time to digest that revelation, but it will be something that will require careful thought and contemplation. "Sweetheart, let's not get ahead of ourselves. Right now, we're on our way to celebrate the blessings bestowed upon Silverstone Bay tonight! You gonna be alright? Be safe. Where are you going?" "I'll be safe mom. We gonna celebrate over at RapCity tonight; we're requested to perform. It seems like everyone is celebrating!" Sixty

B Mackin hugged and kissed his mom; he gave Hercules a brotha dap and parentally said, "I still want to know your intentions with my mother?" then ran off to catch up with his partners.

Hercules escorted Lolena to her car. She waited for him to pull up behind her and they headed to Dominic's. Cruising through the packed parking lot, they found parking spaces on the far side of the lot. Hercules parked his car, jumped out and ran over to open the door for Lolena; they walked into the club hand in hand. Smokey Mike motioned them over to the bar. "Glad to see y'all made it. As you can see, the place is busting at the seams. I reserved a spot over there just for you two. The Brothas are over there; they got started already."

Sherwood and his wife were sitting at the table along with Rafeki and his girlfriend, Nathaniel and his wife; they decided to hang for a little bit before they went home to get rest for the rodeo the next day, and Sonnie was there, but the woman he was with was not his wife. "There they are, glad y'all could make it. We thought you two might've had other ideas for this evening," Sherwood said laughingly. "Well we do have other ideas, but right now we just

13

want to celebrate. Who's buying?" Hercules asked. Sonnie announces, "Drinks are on me." Smokey Mike personally delivered the drinks to the table. "I want to make a toast," Sonnie stands with his drink in the air. "There will never be anybody else in this world that I will ever risk my life for to preserve life, liberty and the pursuit of happiness then this group of distinguished gentleman here." "Here, Here" is said in unison.

Hercules politely asks Sonnie, "who's the lady sitting with you this evening?" "Yes, of course, I had introduced her before you arrived, this is Tiffany Carson; she is here for the weekend. She is out here from Chicago, and we go back to when I played pro basketball; she was one of the cheerleaders. Tiffany, this is Hercules and Lolena." "It's nice to meet you, Tiffany," said Hercules and Lolena nodded her head. "It's a pleasure to finally meet you. Sonnie has told me lots about you." "Well, I trust my Brotha has spoken highly of me then," Hercules says boastfully.

Tiffany was an attractive, coffee colored, five-foot, eight-inch tall woman who had kept her sexy cheerleading body, very well, into her seasoned age. She was polite and seemed real comfortable sitting

14

next to Sonnie in the space normally occupied by his wife. Hercules quickly gave the situation some thought but dismissed any further consideration until another time.

The music was jumping; drinks and food were served nonstop; the dance floor packed, and there were smiles on everyone's face; you heard laughter all around the club, and there was so much conversation going on: "That was the wildest event Silverstone Bay has ever seen." "I knew Jackass Jennings was behind the bullshit that was going on." "I suspected the mayor had something to do with the troubles of the city. There was too much going on not to have corruption at the top." "Thank God; Kayla miraculously returned. I would not have believed anything like that was going to happen. There is truly a God." "There's Lolena. Sista girl is going to be the next mayor of Silverstone Bay." The people there did not interrupt Lolena or the Band of Brothas; the undisturbed time allowed them pure enjoyment and fun.

Hercules whispered to Lolena, "Let's dance." Hercules looked cool, calm and collect; you wouldn't have known that earlier that evening he orchestrated the plan to disrupt the Code Black plan. There were the months of gathering intel; the threats to the lives and livelihood of the people of Silverstone Bay and, foremost, the threat on the life of the woman he loved, which ultimately led to the takedown of the sinister duel, Mr. Ellington and Ballplayer, with the torpedoed football pass of a lifetime.

This extremely cool, confident six-foot, three-inch tall, broad shoulders, muscular arms and legs, six-pack abs, dark chocolate man with the sexy smile dressed in all black finally could dance with the love of his life. Lolena sweetly accepted, "I thought you'd never ask."

What Happened to You that Night?

Hercules and Lolena, hand in hand glided to the packed dance floor. The crowd graciously stepped aside to allow the enchanted couple access to the center of the floor. The fast dance song instinctively changed to a soothing slow song as they made it through the partying citizens of Silverstone Bay. The crowd had something to party about; things would be different, at least, for this moment. Hercules turned to face his love. He had claimed her love. He knew from that moment forward that nothing, or no one, or anything, or anyone would

17

ever get in his way. If something or someone dared to harm, injure, hurt, deceive, betray, abuse or use Lolena Wynn, he or she or it would have to deal with a force of epic proportion.

One in a Million You, sung by Larry Graham, filled the air, Hercules pulled Lolena close. She bumped against his firm six-foot, three-inch, rock-solid frame. He wrapped his herculean arms around her sexy curvy body. She looked sexy in the Silverstone Bay High school colors, red and gold, sweater outfit. After all the events that took place in just one evening, her makeup was flawless. Her luscious red lips looked extremely tasty. Hercules wanted a taste. Lolena wrapped her arms around his shoulders and melted into his manliness. For the next five minutes, Hercules and Lolena were the only couple on the dance floor; the moonlit stars shined down on them; the calm of the night blanketed them with warmth and comfort, the air breezed gently around their bodies. As the song ended, Hercules asked, "What happened to you that night the first time we danced here?" Lolena quickly came back to the moment and recalled the exact moment Hercules asked about, "Hercules, I had to go. Seeing you

18

again, after all that time, was overwhelming in more ways than you think. I took advantage of that second when you turned around and left quickly. Dancing with you that night brought up so many emotions. At first, it didn't even seem real. It felt like some kind of out of body experience. In my wildest dreams, I never thought I would have ever seen you again in my life. Then, there you were. I saw you walk in, I watched you step with your brothas then you disappeared. I had a flashback that you disappeared again out of my life. Anyways, when I saw you later in the evening, I took that moment to, finally, connect with the man that I had loved from afar for so long. And let's not forget the fact that it really had been a very long time since I'd been in the arms of a man especially a man that I loved." Lolena held onto Hercules tighter.

The slow song faded away and then the dance floor started jumpin' again. The old school sounds of Marvin Gaye, Got to Give it Up, excited the dance floor. The dance song went on for twelve minutes, and they repeated it. The partying continued into the wee hours of the morning; dancing, drinking, laughing, eating, talking, kissing hugging and not one ounce of trouble.

The Band of Brotha took over the floor for a few minutes; their signature jam came on, the crowd left the dance floor, and one by one, the brothas stepped to the floor. Smokey Mike stepped out first, "Distinguished Brothas, won't you join me." Hercules, Sherwood, Rafeki, Nathaniel and Sonnie stepped onto the floor. As with all assignments, the Band of Brothas began an assignment with a step march and they ended an assignment with a step march. Smokey Mike signaled the Brothas to start steppin'. They did with the smooth precision exhibited since day one when their united group formed back in the military...One, two step hard One, two step high One, Two kick hop kick high, about face, turnaround step, step, slap left leg, slap right leg, whip up right arm and flick, stop arm high, flick left shoulder, flick right shoulder shimmy shake left, shimmy shake right, whip right arm up folded, lift left leg up, pivot around 180 degrees, put left leg down. Repeat three more times. As with each end of an assignment, they met to debrief. When they ended, they stepped to the back room. The club resumed partying as the Brothas left the floor.

****

Smokey set up the back room; a food platter set in the middle of the conference table; each Brotha's signature, thirst-quenching drink sat on the table waiting for its owner to enjoy after such a dynamic performance. Hercules took a long drink and spoke, "We're not going to take too long. We have more celebrating. We deserve this but let's not kid ourselves; we have to stay ready. Tonight, we put an end to one part of a bigger enigma. The group that began this corruptive scenario here in Silverstone Bay was successful in launching a diabolical plot. We still need to disengage what has started. We were successful in accomplishing tonight's take down of Mr. Ellington, Ball Player and the assassins at the waterfront and at the school, but the source that assisted us over the past months says there is more. Gentleman, I want to introduce you to Philip, Philip Bono was the butler for Mr. Ellington. Unbeknownst to Mr. Ellington and others in that group, Phillip was a highly educated doctor from Eritrea. Mr. Ellington arrogantly assumed he was just a janitor. Anyways,

21

Philip let them all think that. He didn't know where he was going or what would happen, but he agreed to go to America because his grandmother's dying wish was for him to see the world. Gentleman, let's all get to know Philip Bono." Smokey Mike opened the back door and in he walked. Philip walked in the room; he had a little bounce in his step; he smiled and said in a very polished, dignified manner, "Hello my brothas, are you still ready?"

The brothas all stood up, went over to Philip brotha dapped and embraced him. Smokey Mike, "You know we still have work to do." Sonnie, "Thanks, man. We couldn't have done without you." Nathaniel, "Glad to meet you. I know the situation was getting dangerous for you." Sherwood, "Tell us how you kept Kayla safe all this time." Rafeki, "I hear you are the $5.5 million investor in the new Silverstone Bay Hospital."

Phillip felt overwhelmed. The gravity of the situation hit him at that moment. He had been living an imposed lie for ten years. He was separated from his family, his country and his true life for a very long time; he almost forgot who he truly was before the intrusion by Mr. Ellington on his life. Philip was a hardworking doctor at the hospital back in his country. The hospital was small; supplies were often scarce, and the patient load was always high. The country suffered through many years of civil war, and many citizens fled the country. Philip saved as many lives as possible. His grandmother got gravely sick; there wasn't much Phillip could do for her, the hospital had been low on supplies when she came in, but Phillip tried to save her, against all odds. She was old and knew her time was near; Phillip laid at her bedside, she touched her grandson's head, he looked up, tears in his eyes, her parting words, "Go my son, there is a world out there waiting for you" and she closed her eyes.

Phillip looked at the Brothas and said, "Mr. Ellington was the devil walking. As long as he thought he had you under control, you could get close to him. He always assumed everyone was under his control, that how stupid he is. Anyways, he conjured up several plans just in case Code Black didn't work. I fooled him all those years because I spoke very little. I just let him think I didn't speak or understand much English. Hercules he genuinely hates you. He blamed you for ruining his life. What

23

an idiot. The audacity to think another human was a cause of his own woes. He never bothered me. I was able to tolerate his stupidity because just like him, I had to have a plan to live here in America so far away from my homeland. I didn't see any of the destructive things he did over the years, but when he brought little Kayla to the house, it took all my might not to kill him right there. She was so scared. She cried for many days. I would take her food and many times she didn't eat. Then after a few days of not eating much, I fixed her a plate of fun foods, foods, I read children like to eat, fries, hot dogs, chips, ice cream, candy. I sat it on the table in the room and sat down. I started talking about my country and what it was like when I was a little boy. I told her about my sisters and brothers. I told her about my parents and grandparents. I told her how much I missed my family. She listened intently. She started to cry and ran into my arms. She said she wanted her mother and father and grandmother; she was real scared. Then she started talking; she ate the fun food I brought; she was so hungry by then. Then we made a secret pack that night. I told her I would protect her and promised her to get her back to her family.

Nobody ever tried to bother her. They just wanted to keep her until they pulled off the Code Black plan."

Hercules said, "Thank you Philip for being there, for being the man that you are and for helping us save so many lives and the livelihood of Silverstone Bay. Phillip said, "You all are welcome but like I said, there is another plan that will activate if the Code Black plan wasn't successful. My brothas, Code Red is in play."

What Next?

Hercules followed Lolena home from Dominic's. After a long night and now morning of celebrating, the enchanted couple tired, sleepy, and a little tipsy arrived at Lolena's house safe and sound. Hercules walked Lolena to her door; she keyed in her code; he entered her house first, turned on the light, gave her place the Hercules security check, and then he allowed her to enter. She locked her door, looked at him and said, "It is my duty as a concerned citizen not to allow you to get behind the wheel of your car and drive at this time of morning in your condition. You never know if there is a sobriety check point on your way home." She was being flirtatious but serious. She knew he could have easily driven, but she was not ready for the night, well morning, to end just yet. "Can I offer you some tea or something?" Hercules quickly gave the request some thought, "Yes, tea sounds ideal and thank you for your concern on my driving ability, but you don't have to worry, I have that under control." He did not want anything but to wrap his arms around her.

Hercules sat on the couch and waited for Lolena to return. She yelled from the kitchen, "I put the teapot on and would you excuse me while I slip into something more comfortable; it won't take but a few minutes." "Take your time, I am very comfortable sitting right here," he responded through a small yawn. When Lolena entered the living room carrying a serving tray, she saw Hercules comfortably positioned with his head tilted back, one arm resting on the back and the other arm resting on the armrest of her overstuffed red couch, fast asleep. She stared at him for a minute. She set the tray down on the table. As she set it down, he opened his eyes, sat up and gently grabbed her hips and pulled her down next to him. She had slipped on a silk, floor-length, beautifully designed dashiki; she sprayed a little

27

perfume on, and had let her hair down. She felt so soft, silky and sexy to him. He looked at her through his sleepy eyes; she was a vision of beauty. He sexily muttered, "Excuse me sweetheart, I just closed my eyes for a minute and must have fallen asleep. When I opened my eyes and saw this beautiful woman bending in front of me, I was unable to control myself, and I had to grab you. Please excuse my forwardness." She smoothly positioned herself wrapped in his arms and put her head on his shoulders and went to sleep. He kissed her on her head and went back to sleep himself.

Lolena sat up quickly. She turned and saw Hercules was still there, sleeping. She looked down and saw that he was ready. At some point after they fell asleep, Hercules had unbuttoned his pants, nested his right hand inside his pants, and he was holding his long, thick, obviously erect love stick. He slowly opened his eyes; he didn't say anything; she didn't say anything. He sat up and looked at her. She stood up and removed her silk dashiki. He stood up, removed his black shirt, tossed it on the chair and took her in his arms. He kissed her softly on her lips, then her cheeks and began to move down to her neck.

28

He sat down and positioned her in front of him. He kissed and sucked her breast, licked down to her naval and stopped. He stood up, tilted her chin up, looked into her eyes and asked, "Are you ready?" She mumbled, "I was ready a long time ago." He sat down, resumed licking her around her naval, and then moved his hot tongue into her hot spot. He licked, sucked, and then made his long tongue lick in and out of her wet, juicy, hot vagina. His tongue moved in and out as if it were a rock hard penis. She watched his movements, listened to his moaning and growling, and held onto his shoulders with all her might. "Hercules, Hercules, Hercules don't let go, you're making me come." Lolena heard the front key code entered. The doorknob was turning.

Lolena sat up quickly because she heard someone at her front door. She snapped out of her dream state. She looked down and saw she still had her silk dashiki on; she whipped her head around and saw Hercules still sleeping, but he opened his eyes because he, also, heard the door opening. *"I was dreaming, that was a dream, it felt so real," she thought.* Her heart was beating fast; her face felt quite warm. Hercules looked at her and asked,

"Baby, are you okay; you look a little shaken?" She didn't respond.

It was daylight in the early morning, and Sixty B Mackin came walking in the door. He looked and saw his mother and Hercules looking at him. "Man, this feels like déjà vu," he exclaimed. "Didn't I catch you two in this same position before? I thought y'all were going to get a room to handle your business," he said. "This is déjà vu alright, and like the last time, you so called caught us in this position I said Boy, what are you doing coming in this time of the morning?" His mother said. "Okay, mom, it may be a little early in the morning but this time I have justifiable reasons for steppin' in this time of the morning." "You do? Well, state your case but shut the door." "Ok, I'll shut the door but can I bring in a friend of mine?" Lolena grimaced at her son and asked, "Who?" "I met her last night at RapCity. She was one of the lucky ladies that were able to sit with us in the VIP section. Can I go get her and bring her in before we start talking?" "Go on, bring her in," Lolena permitted.

Lolena turned to Hercules and inquired how he slept, "Looks like we spent the night on this couch again. You're not too stiff are you?" "No, I slept like a baby. All I needed was you in my arms," he said as he squeezed her. "Well, I must agree with you. That was the best sleep I had since the last time I slept in your arms. *And that was the best dream I ever had*," she agreed and decided to keep her dream to herself for the moment.

Alvin aka Sixty B Mackin came in, and he brought his friend in and introduced Sheila Hedgepeth to his mother and Hercules. She was a petite young lady with big eyes, long eyelashes; caramel colored and stood only five feet tall. "Mom, this is Sheila. She is one of my fans," Sixty said that last part jokingly. "We met last night. She says she has been following my music, and she wanted a chance to, possibly, record a duet with me. She thinks we could make a beautiful love song. Sheila, this is my beautiful mother, Ms. Wynn, and this is Detective McMarshall." "Well, Sheila it's nice to meet you. Why are you two out at this time in the morning?" Lolena tersely replied. Sheila spoke in her soft, sweet voice, "Please forgive me, us, for our unprofessional behavior. It is very nice to meet you Ms. Wynn and you, Detective McMarshall. I told

Alvin to wait for a more appropriate time." "Alvin, Alvin? You called my son Alvin," Lolena shockingly said. "I thought he forgot his real name, running around here referring to himself as Sixty B Mackin. Thank you, young lady for referring to him by his birth name. Well, if he told you his name is Alvin, he must see something special in you. Oh my goodness, come on in here and sit down. I would like to get to know you a little bit more." The young couple sat down. Hercules acknowledged the young lady and sat down. "So, where have y'all been all night? Alvin, you know I don't want you out in the streets all hours in the night." "Mom, I can take care of myself. You taught me well. Especially now, things are going to be changing," Sixty said sincerely. "I know it's real early in the morning, but there are some things I want to tell you now and I'm glad you are here Detective McMarshall. Last night at RapCity, all people were talking about were the events at the game. The place with packed. People came there from everywhere, seems like. The main thing everyone was talking about was the way the city wants to elect you to be the mayor of Silverstone Bay. All of a sudden, things started getting all-political. People were coming up with slogans: We Win with Wynn, Let Lolena Lead, Write in Wynn. Those were some of the better ones. Now you know RapCity is a hip-hop club; most of the people are way under the age of thirty, but tonight, they were in there forming committees to help with the campaign. A lot of the people there were also at the game; when they watched that video and heard the plan to bring in a private prison complex to lock us up. We ain't havin' that! So Mom, we want to help on the campaign."

Lolena was stunned. She sat on the couch and listened to her son talk about campaigning, and wanting to help and singing love songs and referring to himself by his birth name. "Well, this all sounds extremely intriguing, What Next?" "Well we were thinking about hosting a few campaign events at RapCity. The owner Peace B Out and I have gotten pretty tight since we performed there a few months ago and turned the place out. Mom, we have to clean up our city and what better way to help clean up then by using the people who made it dirty." "Son, I am so proud of you, but let's not get ahead of ourselves. I haven't made any decisions yet. There is so much to

33

consider. First, we have to do our homework and determine the responsibilities of a mayor and the possibilities of me being able to pull it off. This is real serious stuff." "I know, Mom by I'm, we, are going to be right there with you. Oh yeah, last night I saw this guy, this white guy and he was with the woman wearing a very, very, tight, red dress. I would not have paid attention to them, but I remember the guy with at RapCity the night we performed, and he was with Ball Player. I put two and two together, and I conclude he's, probably, some of the trash we need to clean up."

We Have a Rodeo to Attend

"Well, this has been an extremely, wonderful conversation with you, son. We are going to continue it later. Now, go get some rest. We have a rodeo to attend this afternoon; will you and your friend be coming?" Lolena asked Alvin. "That sounds like it could be fun. Sheila would you like to go to a rodeo today?" Alvin asked. Sheila quickly answered, "Yes, I've never been to a rodeo before. Sounds like fun." "I will text you the location, it is about twenty miles north of Silverstone Bay," Lolena informed her son and his friend. Alvin and Sheila left the room.

Hercules spoke soon after they left the room, "Sweetheart, I think I am good to drive now, so I am going to go, freshen up and be back to pick you up in a couple of hours." Hercules wanted to take Lolena to her bedroom and make passionate love to her, but things had changed suddenly. Lolena stared at Hercules a little bit before she spoke, "Okay, that sounds like a plan. Can I offer you some coffee, tea or me?" That offer stopped him in his tracks. "Well, of course, I will have option three and I would like it slow, hot, and I will probably want a second helping," he said as he wrapped his arms around her. She giggled as he kissed her on her neck. "And, since we aren't alone anymore, can I take a rain check on that offer?" he whispered in her ear. "Yes, and that rain check is good until redeemed," and she sealed that deal with a kiss.

Hercules left and texted the Brothas the newly acquired intel provided by Sixty B Mackin who will probably revert to using his birth name, Alvin Wynn. A truly good woman can change a man overnight. *"That young man has a lot of heart, and he loves his mother so much. I will take him out and let him know my intentions with his mother," Hercules thought.*

It was a beautiful sunny day for a rodeo. Nathaniel was at the stables early that morning. He loved to ride his horse, Black Bucket; he takes every opportunity to get to the stables. Today was the Annual Black Cowboy Rodeo Show for Northern California. Cowboys and Cowgirls, from all around the country, register to participate. The show exhibits the superior riding abilities of the participants. When the show begins, first, the lone cowboy rides down the hill carrying an American flag, as a long, allegiance-type address fills the air, all the participants, then, ride into the arena sitting tall on the backs of huge horses of all the colors: white, brown, black, red. The extremely experienced riders can make their horses dance. The crowd immensely enjoyed it when the cowboys rode swiftly around the arena; you get a sense of what it was like back in the real cowboy days. Along with the real cowboys performing, the crowd could be cowboys for a day; everyone has the opportunity to wear cowboy hats, boots and cowboy attire. Along with watching exciting horse riding, the food vendors keep the crowd scrumptiously fed all day.

Hercules and Lolena arrived much earlier than most of the crowd. Nathaniel advised everyone the earlier the better since the show always sold out. They met Sherwood and his wife, Stephanie, Rafeki

37

and his girlfriend, Kena, Smokey Mike and his wife, Zelma and Sonnie with the friend from Chicago, Tiffany. Sonnie was actually wearing a cowboy hat instead of his headdress of choice, a fedora. Lolena's son, Alvin and his new friend, Sheila wore cowboy hats; they walked around, holding hands, eating a little bit of everything. Lolena introduced her son to everyone, "this is my son, Alvin, some call him Sixty B Mackin, and this is his friend Sheila. This is their first rodeo; may be after watching Nathaniel performed, they might want to become riders." "Mom, that's not even funny, but it does look pretty cool. Nice to meet everyone," Alvin said, and Sheila concurred. "Okay, Mom I will see you later," and kissed her on the cheek.

It was Nathaniel's time to perform; he looked very tall sitting up on his horse, Black Bucket. The riding duet sprinted around the arena and had the fastest time. Later, during the rodeo-riding relay, their team took first place. All the participants put on a phenomenal show.

During the intermission, the Brothas went to get food and drink. Hercules asked, "Did y'all get the text this morning? I know that's not enough to find this guy and throw him in jail, but we have to pursue the information." Rafeki said, "I'll talk with the owner of RapCity. He was very helpful with the intel before." "Speaking of RapCity, the young man you just met, Lolena's son, he said RapCity is about to become the campaign headquarters for Lolena should she actually decide to fill the vacant mayor seat." "That sounds very interesting, is she going to do it?" Rafeki asked. "Well, it's been less than twenty-four hours since the town self-elected her for the position. She barely has had any time to think about everything that has happened let alone running for the position of mayor of Silverstone Bay. That's a big responsibility," Hercules answered. "If you think about it just a little, she'd be an extraordinary mayor. She's a pretty dynamic woman. If anybody knows that, it's you, Herc. You should get her to think about it. There's not a lot of time till Election Day," Sherwood said. "I know she would have almost 100% of the city's support. She could build a strong cabinet. She could clean up city hall. Silverstone Bay has a mess to clean up. We were left in the dark for so long, no tellin' how many backroom deals were made under the leadership of that crooked Mayor Burton," Sherwood concluded.

Hey Sonnie, I see your wife didn't accompany you today. What's goin' on? You and Stacy are our version of the Cosby's. I mean is there anything you want to share with your Brothas?" Smokey Mike inquired. All the Brothas anxiously waited for Sonnie to give a response. They knew Sonnie loved his wife deeply, but they were surprised to meet Sonnie's out of town guest, Tiffany, at Dominic's last night. Sonnie stood quietly for a few seconds before he said, "Yes, of course, I love Stacy. You know, we've been inseparable since we met back when I played pro ball." He gave a short laugh. "Lord knows she had to put up with me on more than one occasion. A pro basketball player is tempted 24/7. The team travels to different cities; we are traveling with the cheerleaders; many of the cheerleaders have a mission to land a ballplayer. Stacy was a cheerleader for a short time, but she quit the squad. I didn't know her when she was a cheerleader. I met her at a team event; we hit it off and been inseparable ever since. Since I found my true love mate, it seemed to create an invisible barrier around me; women didn't have the same effect on me anymore. I started seeing the cheerleaders as my little sisters, and I would watch out for them to keep them

40

out of trouble. Anyways, Tiffany and I became real good friends, and there was never any sexual attraction. We stayed friends. She called and said she was coming to California for business and wanted to come and visit. She's going through a messy divorce." "Does Stacy approve of this brother/sister relationship?" Smokey asked. "Stacy and Tiffany were friends before we met." Sonnie stopped talking and stared back at the crowd. "Tiffany will be leaving today. Her flight is later this evening. She confided some disturbing news to me on our way over here. Man, it threw me for a few loops." He stopped talking. The Brothas looked at him waiting for him to finish his story.

Before Sonnie resumed talking, there was a commotion in the bleachers over were the women were sitting. There was a large congregation of people gathering in the area, and more people kept moving in that direction. The Brothas ran back to see what was going on. They had difficulty making their way through the crowd. They heard the crowd shout out things like: Lolena you have to take the mayor position. Have you decided to run? We are here to support you. Lolena! Can you do something about the prison that is going to be built at the old military

41

base? The Brothas had to get their ladies out of the stands. It was difficult because the crowd was getting thicker with each person moving in that direction.

Nathaniel saw the commotion in the stands. He spotted his Brothas attempting to work their way through the crowd. He knew he had to go into Ready mode. Nathaniel instructed a couple of his cowboy friends to follow him. They rode over to the crowd and rode the horses up into the stands. When the people saw the horses come in their direction, they quickly moved out of the way. The crowd thinned quickly. As the crowd thinned, the Brothas made it to their women, grab their hands and followed Nathaniel and the small posse back to the stables.

I'm Going to be the Mayor of Silverstone Bay

Lolena opened her eyes. The room was dark. Panic consumed her body. She sat up quickly, looked around and realized she was in her bed. She felt her body, and she was fully clothed. She looked around, she didn't hear anything, looked at the clock, "3:00? What happened? Where is? What happened?" She was confused, the last thing she remembered was being at the rodeo, there was a large crowd; so many people were around her asking her questions, hugging her, pulling her in different directions. Then she remembered seeing Nathaniel sitting on his horse, Hercules picked her up and after that, things got fuzzy. Lolena got out of bed and walked downstairs, Hercules was sleep on the couch and

Alvin was sleep on the loveseat. She let them sleep and went back upstairs; she needed to think about what happened.

For a few seconds, Lolena had a horrible flashback of the morning she woke up after the, God forsaken night, when fellow soldiers raped her when she was in the military. She had to rebuild herself after that traumatic event. The military discharged her and gave her a few thousand dollars allotment with the explicit orders never to talk about what happened to her to anyone. She didn't ever talk about it again; over twenty years passed before she ever mentioned it again and that was to Hercules. As she reflected back on her life since that point, she can see the different points in her life when the effects of that night took its toll on her.

Lolena's marriage to Alvin's father suffered, sometimes unjustifiably because she could not trust men, intimacy, commitment, government, authority, etc. She was so young when the rape happened. When she left the military, she went back to her hometown. She lived at home for a few months. Her mother came to her one day, and out of the blue, she said, "What doesn't kill you makes you stronger." Her mother didn't ask Lolena any questions on why

44

she was no longer in the military. After she told her that, she hugged and told her, "I will always be with you even when you are not in my presence; now go do some good." Lolena moved shortly after that, enrolled in college, received her undergrad and graduate degrees, met her husband at the mall, married him six months later, her son was born a year later. She stayed married for eleven years and her husband came to her one day and said, "I am not happy, I filed for divorce; we have a court date on Wednesday." The shock of that announcement from her ex-husband didn't kill her; her mother was right, but her mother didn't say anything about killing someone who pissed her off. What pissed Lolena the most was that she should have been the one filing for divorce; there had been enough reasons to divorce him, but Lolena was the kind of woman that committed herself to marriage; her parents were still married after seven children, fourteen grandchildren and forty-two years of marriage. However, Lolena's ex-husband was no prince charming, except for the first time she met him. He turned out to be a jack-of-all-trades, master of none, a cheater, liar, womanizer, and an absentee husband and dad.

Lolena's head felt like it was spinning as if she was riding a roller coaster. She heard voices in her head. The feeling of euphoria hit her, *"I love you, Lolena";* then a feeling of exhaustion, *"Where am I?";* then excitement, *"Lolena Wynn Write Her In!";* then despair, *"you are being discharged from the military";* then excitement, *"Mom, we will help you";* then anger, *"I was raped";* then hope, *"What doesn't kill you makes you stronger."* At that moment, Lolena had an epiphany.

Earlier at the rodeo during the intermission, a few people came up to her and asked if she was going to run for mayor since the audience self-elected her at the game. Then more people came asking the same questions and offering their support. Then more people came and started asking what was she was going to do about the problems in Silverstone Bay as if she was already the mayor of the city. Then she heard people say, "Lolena Wynn is over here." A few people asked if they could take a picture with her. Then several people started taking pictures. Poor Stephanie, Kena, Zelma and Tiffany, the people crowded in on their space. They all were terribly uncomfortable with the throng of people sucking all the air out of the area and creating an extraordinarily claustrophobic atmosphere. It was becoming unbearable then at that second Hercules picked Lolena up and carried her to safety. He came to her rescue again. *"I am going to be the Mayor of Silverstone Bay," whispered Lolena.*

Lolena opened her eyes; it was daylight; there was a knock at her door. "Come In." Hercules slowly opened the door and looked at her, "Well, Good Morning My Queen. You should be well rested." "Good Morning My Hero. Looks like you saved me again," Lolena said in a low, smooth tone." "You fell asleep on the way home yesterday, I carried you up here to bed; you never opened your eyes. I checked to make sure you were still breathing. I ended up sleeping back on your couch again. I wasn't going to leave you by yourself. The way that crowd acted yesterday, I had to make sure they didn't follow us home and start knocking at your door. Your son was so worried about you. He stood guard with me." Hercules was sitting on her bed now rubbing her legs. "Yeah, I saw how well you two were guarding me this morning around 3:00," she said sarcastically teasing him about being sleep at his post. "You and Alvin were quite comfortable." "We must've just fallen asleep. The house was secure at that time," he said as he continued to rub her legs. He looked up and down the silhouette of her body under the Kenta-cloth designed blanket. "Baby, you know you don't have to worry about anything, I got you," as he squeezed her leg. "And, that's why I am going to be the mayor of Silverstone Bay," she said with a huge smile.

Hercules stopped rubbing Lolena's leg; he looked at with piercing eyes and asked her to say what he thought he heard her say again, "Come again?" "You heard me, I'm going to be the mayor of Silverstone Bay," she repeated. "That's what I thought you said." Hercules was silent. There was a knock at the door. "Come in," Lolena said as she set up in bed. "Good Morning Mom. Are you okay?" asked Alvin as he came around to the other side of the bed and kissed her on her cheek. "Yes, sweetheart, I'm fine, and I'm going to be the next mayor of Silverstone Bay," she said to her son who looked seriously concerned at that moment. Then his expression changed to excitement, "That's what I'm talking about. You gon' be the mayor of Silverstone Bay! I know it got pretty wild yesterday at the rodeo, but that's alright, we gotcha. Nobody is going to crowd you like that again. You should have seen how

Hercules and the Brothas got y'all outta there. Brotha Nate was sitting up on his horse, Big Bucket, and that's all it took; when those people saw that horse, they moved!" Alvin gladly gave his mother blow-by-blow details of yesterday's events.

Due Diligence

Lolena, Hercules, and Alvin had breakfast. It had been a while since she'd cooked a Sunday breakfast for her family. They consumed home fries, cheesy eggs, turkey patties, cinnamon buns, and fresh-squeezed orange juice until they were way past full. Alvin left to meet his new friend and tell her that his mother was going to be the mayor of Silverstone Bay.

After Lolena and Hercules cleaned the country-styled kitchen, they retreated outside to the backyard. Her backyard was her private oasis; she'd sit out there and have a mini stay-cation whenever she felt the mood. The sun warmed the air to an ideal tropical temperature that allow the enchanted couple to spend time quietly together because life was about to get extremely hectic in more ways than they could imagine at that moment. Lolena laid back on her floral-design cushioned lounge chair, and for the first time ever, Hercules was with her, he pulled the other lounge chair right next to hers and stretched out next to the woman of his dream. His heart consumed with strong feelings of joy, happiness, love and lust. The more time he spent with her in close proximity, the more his desire for her heated up. They laid there in silence for a long while; before you knew it, they fell asleep. Hercules woke first. He felt well rested when he opened his eyes. Lolena was still sleeping, her eyes were flickering; she snored softly. He thought about how he didn't tell her how her life was in danger and through the grace of God, she is okay. There she was; asleep in her backyard; probably dreaming about being the mayor of Silverstone Bay, however, it may not be a dream, there is a strong possibility it will be so.

It was just a couple of days ago when the Band of Brothas foiled a ridiculous plot to take over Silverstone Bay via a plan called Code Black. Ridiculous as that plan was, the reality is that lives were threatened, and lives were lost. Lolena's life was threatened. Now, there is another plan dubbed Code Red. The Band of Brothas had to stay ready now that Lolena was going to be a public official. Yesterday the situation had gotten completely out of control. The people had good intentions, but the town is still on edge because too many things had happened. Hercules sat quietly watching and thinking, *"How am I going to keep you safe, my love."*

Lolena opened her eyes, Hercules was staring at her, and then he smiled. "I thought I was dreaming about sitting in my backyard lying next to you, but I'm not, there you are staring at me. How long have you been looking at me?" Lolena asked as she stretched. "Well, sweetheart, I have been gazing at you for a little while and thinking about you and your decision to be the mayor of Silverstone Bay," replied Hercules. "Don't get me wrong, you will be a phenomenal mayor; that goes without saying, I'm just thinking of your safety. Yesterday, the people at the rodeo had good intentions, but things got out of hand so quickly. The people there have love for you, but that is not always going to be the case. You have to change your whole life style effective

52

immediately. This might be the last time you can just lay out in your backyard and just kick it."

No sooner than Hercules completed that sentence, they heard cars driving up; car horns blaring; car doors slamming as people got out and ran towards Lolena's house; Hercules's cell phone rang; dogs started barking from the neighbors backyards; the doorbell rang; they could hear people saying, "Is she home?" "Knock on the door!" "Hey, Lolena Wynn, are you home?" The doorbell continued to ring. Lolena and Hercules heard a much louder noise, it sounded like a helicopter; they looked up in the sky, there was a helicopter approaching from the north, and it hovered over the house. They looked up in utter amazement and quickly ran into the house.

****

Jennifer Jason and Mr. G flew into San Francisco late Friday night. They checked in the Fairmount Inn in Brisbane, a city ten miles south of the city and ten miles north of Silverstone Bay. "This is a purrrfit location to stay while we complete the Code Red plan," she said as the r's rolled off her tongue. "We have time before we go to that club, RapCity, for you to come over here, snatch this T-shirt and leggings off and ram your cock in my...well,

I'll let you decide where you want to put it," she commanded as spread her legs and leaned back against the desk chair positioned in front of the mirror in the eloquently-designed suite. Mr. G didn't say a word, he put his gun back in his holster, unzipped his pants, removed his cock, jerk it a few times, held his hard sausage in his hand as he walked over to her. She wanted him to take her from behind, she turned and faced the mirror; he came up to her, ripped her leggings off, used his left hand and grabbed her breast, bent down a little and rammed his cock into her, hard, "there you go, take it hard, take it hard." He pounded her hard for minutes, he was so excited, she was in another state of ecstasy; he had the ability to get her there quickly, he pulled out and jerked his load on her back, "now, turn around and suck the rest of this come out of me." She obeyed him and got down on her knees, licked and sucked his cock as if it was a lollipop.

Since Keith Jason, her husband was dead, but it had been less than twenty-four hours, Jennifer felt relieved now that she could allow Mr. G to sex her at any given moment. They dressed and made their way to RapCity. Mr. G wanted to speak with the owner about a few things. The hip-hop club was packed;

they were still able to get in. He remembered the place from a few months ago when he went there with Mr. Ellington, Keith Jason and Ball Player. He was there for the Code Black plan, now it's the Code Red plan. Jennifer squeezed into a tight red dress; the dress was probably one of the reasons they were able to get into the filled-to-capacity establishment. The deceitful couple, however, looked out of place, but no one bothered them; they didn't go unnoticed, nonetheless.

The RapCity crowd was celebrating the events of that evening, and Mr. G and Jennifer heard the talk about electing Lolena Wynn as the mayor of Silverstone Bay. "This can't happen, this can't be," whispered Mr. G. "We were supposed to have had Burton in that position. We're going to have to make sure that doesn't happen," he leaned over and kissed Jennifer on the lips.

****

Mr. G and Jennifer were amongst the crowd that was now gathering around Lolena's house. The crowd grew larger by the minute. The media started the frenzy. They smelled a sensational story, a real powerful story. They got wind of the explosive events that happened at the football game where the top city officials were exposed on video tape as part of the masterminds behind the criminal activity that had been taking place in Silverstone Bay. The most recent case of the high school coach, Andrew Michaels, blatantly gunned down in front of his house and his family was just inside; that murder made national news, and now the city is thrust back into the headlines, again. At that event, the town citizens witnessed their mayor and chief of police handcuffed and taken away by the FBI. Minutes after that, the citizens there unanimously, by verbal expression, elected Lolena Wynn to be the write-in mayoral candidate.

Jennifer looked at Lolena's house. At that moment, the door opened, and Lolena stepped out; standing right next to her was Hercules McMarshall. Her heart dropped, she felt a stabbing sensation in her head and sweat beaded on her forehead. *"There he was after all these years, and he stood next to that woman. You won't turn me down this time, I promise you," thought Jennifer as she stared at the two.*

****

Lolena and Hercules stood in the kitchen; they listened to all the commotion; the noise was getting louder; they could tell more and more people were gathering outside. Hercules hugged Lolena, and she hugged him back. He stepped back, looked her up and down, took her back in his arms and kissed her. Her lips parted, and she allowed his hot tongue to penetrate her mouth. He tasted good; she tasted good. They stood in the kitchen passionately kissing while the world was clamoring to get in, to get to them; they knew that everything was about to get real.

"Baby, what do you want to do," Hercules simply asked. He knew life was no longer going to be simple. "Well, I'm going to, first, pray. Here, hold my hand, Dear Lord; I come to you for your guidance, love and support. I know you will be my rock. Amen. Second, due diligence is in order; we have some homework to do; research on: What are the responsibilities of a mayor?" Third, let's go out here, say hello and get these un-invited guests outta here," she says sass in her voice and swagger in her stride.

What Is Phillip Going to do With His Life?

Kayla was home, now. She had been missing for two years, three months, fourteen days, seventeen hours and twenty-six minutes according to the digital counter on the wall. Donald Spencer, Kayla's dad started counting the days, hours and minutes from the first day she went missing. Day One, he made a pledge to God and himself that if the universe would be so kind to return his daughter back in his arms; to the people who loved her the most, he would never give up hope that she would return safe and sound. He made that pledge because on that day, he would have killed someone with his bare hands to find his daughter. He had to find a way to save himself from

58

the brink of insanity that he felt as each minute ticked by, and his daughter was not home with him, her mother and her grandmother.

Donald Spencer was a thirty-seven year old, five feet, ten-inch tall, fare skinned, slim-built man. He wore a fade cut and a few strands of grey sprinkled through the top of his head. He was a science graduate from San Francisco State, and he had worked with a San Francisco science laboratory since he graduated from college; he moved to Silverstone Bay after college. He met his wife, Donna Spencer, in college, she grew up in Silverstone Bay, and they moved there after graduation. The house they lived in belonged to his wife's family for generations.

Donna Spencer was a petite, five-foot, three-inch tall, fare complexion, pretty woman. She was pregnant when Kayla was kidnapped; she almost miscarried, twice. The whole ordeal took its toll on her. She gave birth to a healthy, seven-pound baby boy, his twin didn't make it; another victim of the corrupt Code Black plan. The surviving twin named Kyle Spencer. Kayla didn't know her mother was pregnant at the time she was taken; it was going to be a surprise announcement that traumatic day. Kayla's grandmother didn't even know her daughter was pregnant. That evening, it was going to be a grand announcement, *"Kayla, mom, we have a surprise for you...there is going to be a new member in the house in about eight months!"* That announcement was never made; grandma didn't find out her daughter was pregnant until the day she was rushed to the hospital on the verge of a miscarriage.

Grandma was a spiritual woman. She was at the age where she spent much of her time at the church. She and her friends like to surf the internet. They didn't have internet back in their day. They would all go to the senior center and spend hours on the internet. She will come home with some fascinating story about what she found of the internet: "You can lose twenty pounds in twenty days" "the human camera," "foods you should eat to live a long life," and all the pictures and videos you can now see on the internet. She had an extensive collection of pictures of President Obama and the first family. She never thought in her lifetime that she'd ever ever ever vote for a black man to be president, and he would win! That was a glorious day for her, November 4, 2008 President Barack Obama the declared winner. She held onto moments like that to give her strength; her granddaughter was missing. She didn't know how many days she had ahead of her and every day that Kayla was missing, was one less day she would be able to spend with her granddaughter; she lost two years, three months, fourteen days, seventeen hours and twenty-six minutes. Time she would never get back. She didn't dwell on that fact; it was the reality of the situation. Grandma Veronica Grayson was a beautiful, spunky, sixty-eight year old widow. Her husband past ten years earlier and she wasn't interested in replacing him. She did visit a few internet-dating sites, but she stayed away from actually going through with any chance of ever meeting anyone. Kayla stayed in Grandma's prayers. She devoted as much time as she could helping her daughter with baby Kyle. Donna Spencer stayed strong as she could during the ordeal. She had bouts with depression; having her mother there was a saving grace. She kept Donna focused; she would remind her, "Baby, your baby will come home. The Lord and I are in communication about that. You are going to stay strong for baby Kyle. He is our blessing. He is here to keep us together. Everything is going to be alright."

Donald called Smokey Mike that morning, "Hey Smokey, this is Donald Spencer." Smokey was at Dominic's handling business; he had his cleaning crew in, spit shinning every glass, counter, mirror, table, chair, floor, carpet, door, toilet, sink, window, stove, refrigerator, bar, anything and everything in the place. All the windows and doors were opened to allow the breeze in to sweep the air. There was a crew cleaning the parking lot and tightening up the landscaping. Smokey was in his office when Donald called, "Well what's up. It's good to hear from you. You must be still walking on Cloud Nine now that your baby girl is back home." "God is good...that's why I'm calling. I want to thank you, everyone who helped get my baby girl back home...I want especially to thank Phillip. I understand you know how I can get in touch with him." Donald said. "That I do. He would like that. He even said that. So let's make that all happen. I can bring him over to your house. Is that okay?" Smokey replied. "Yes, do you think he would like to come today?" Donald asked. "I can't speak for him, but I am sure it won't be too much of a problem. I'll get back with 'cha shortly," Smokey hung up, called Phillip and the meeting was set.

62

Phillip was in seclusion. The Brothas felt it would be best if he remained out of site. The situation was still hot, and Phillip had no place else to go; he actually could have been considered a hostage, himself. Mr. Ellington brought him over from Eritrea, but he was thousands of miles away from his family and country; now that Phillip was a free man, what was he going to do with his life? Under the confines of Mr. Ellington, he did get his citizenship. The only family Phillip had was Mr. Black, the black Chihuahua that belonged to Mr. Ellington. Mr. Black dis-owned Mr. Ellington years ago; in his little dog's brain, Phillip was his master. Phillip, Kayla and Mr. Black actually became a family away from their family. Phillip was able to gain Kayla's trust; she saw that he would protect her and return her to her family; because of Phillip's devotion to protecting her, she probably won't experience too much PTSD. The phone rang. "Hello...Oh, Mr. Smokey Mike, it's good to hear from you...Ok, Smokey...Yes, I am doing well. I am watching TV, eating, sleeping. What do you call it? I am being a 'couch potato'. Ha Ha Ha...Yes, Yes, I would love to see Kayla and meet her family. I feel I already know them...Yes, I will be ready. See you soon."

63

Smokey Mike and Phillip arrived at the Spencer's house later that afternoon. Phillip brought Mr. Black along; he thought Kayla would like to see him; the two were inseparable during her two-year captivity. They knocked on the front door; they heard someone running to the door and Kayla sprung the door open and jumped in Phillip's arms. Mr. Black jumped up and down, wagging his tail; barking for Kayla's attention. Donald stood at the door watching with amazement, his daughter so happy to see Phillip. It brought a smile to his face and tears to his eyes. Kayla bent down and played with Mr. Black, "Hi Mr. Black, how are you doing! Good Boy." The black Chihuahua panted around in circles; tail wagging, so excited to see his little friend. Everyone went inside. When Phillip stepped inside, a strong sense of familiarity hit him hard. Donald looked at Phillip for the first time up close and personal; he looked Phillip up and down and then straight in his eyes. "I am so glad to meet you and thank you for keeping my daughter safe. Please excuse me for looking at you so strangely, but I feel I 've met you." Phillip exchanged the same piercing stare and said, "You are welcome, I protected your daughter as if she were my own. I would have killed someone if

64

anyone tried to harm her. Kayla is a beautiful girl; I promise you, she will be alright. I told her every day that her parents are looking for her and one day you all would be together again." As Donald listened to Phillip speak, his accent sounded remarkably familiar, "You have a very familiar accent, where you from?" "That is the first time I have been asked that question since I came to this country. I am from Eritrea, it's a small country that borders..." "Ethiopia, I know where Eritrea is located," Donald interrupts, "I know exactly where Eritrea is, my father is from there." "Did you say he's from there?" Phillip asked as his eyes widened. "I can't believe this, what is your father's name?" "His American name is Steven Spencer; he changed it when he got to this country because it was easier for Americans to pronounce, but his birth name is Stepian Bonneagean." Phillip's heart skipped beats; it felt like his head was spinning; he couldn't believe what he just heard. He, too, changed his name to make it easier to pronounce Bonneagean. "I changed my name for the same reason; my birth name is Phelean Bonneagean." The two men stood there, slightly shocked, Kayla and Smokey Mike looked at them, Mr. Black's tail stopped wagging, and he stared at

65

them. "My father had a brother named Stephian; because of the civil wars, many families were separated, he lost touch with him many, many years ago," Philip said when he was able to speak again. "My father told me he lost contact with his family because he came to this country when he was real young. Spencer was the name of the family that took him in," said Donald when he was able to speak again. The revelation hit the two men; they were cousins, decedents of the Bonneagean family of Eritrea. Phillip had been protecting Kayla Spencer who was his second cousin on his father side of the family. Everyone standing there erupted in tremendous jubilation!

The excitement brought Donna Spencer, carrying Baby Kyle and Grandma into the foyer. "What's all the excitement, it sounds like music to my ears to hear such a joyful noise," inquired Grandma. "God is continuing to bless us, Sweetheart, Grandma this man standing here is Phillip, the man who kept Kayla safe while she was away from us. We just discovered we are cousins; our dads are brothers!" Donna and Grandma stood shocked; they looked with tears in their eyes at Phillip, speechless. Phillip went to them and hugged them. "Who is this?" Phillip asked. "Phillip, Phillip while I was gone, I got a new baby brother; his name is Kyle," answered Kayla with big sisterly pride. Phillip took Kyle in his arms, hugged his little cousin and wept.

You're Coming Home With Me

The crowd outside Lolena's house did not go away even after she went out and said, "I am sure you have questions about what my intentions regarding the upcoming election. There will be a press conference this week regarding that and the events that took place at Silverstone High School. It would be in everyone's best interest to hold your questions till that time. Thank you and please be careful leaving this area." Three hours later there was still a crowd camped outside her house; most of the vehicles parked as not to obstruct traffic; there were two police cops directing traffic at opposite ends of the street.

"You know my neighbors are wondering what's going on," said Lolena as she peeked out of one of the upstairs windows. "You're coming home with me. Staying here right now is too unstable; too much can go wrong," said Hercules authoritatively. Lolena did not challenge Hercules' decision. "Okay, what's the plan?" She said. "Here, send this text to your son, I will make some calls, pack enough items for at least two weeks, call your neighbors and be ready to go in forty-five minutes."

Lolena sent the text to her son; she called her neighbors and she packed. Thirty minutes later a white limo drove up in front of Lolena's house; out stepped Sixty B Mackin and the J-Knock Ent. crew. The media started taking pictures and hollered out questions, "What brings your group to Ms. Wynn's house today?" "Can I get a statement?" "What is your relationship with Ms. Wynn?" The group didn't stop, didn't answer a question, and didn't look at anyone. Hercules opened the door without them knocking.

Lolena ran and embraced her son. There were six members of his group with him and his new friend, Sheila; she walked in with them wearing a hoodie and baggy jeans. "Thank you, Sheila for doing this for me, here are the clothes you will wear,"

69

Lolena gave her a long skirt, tank top, five-inch high black stilettos and a shawl that wrapped over her head and around her body. Sheila went and put on the outfit, and when she walked back in the room, she looked like Lolena standing there. The wrap hid her face so you wouldn't have known it wasn't Lolena walking out of the house. "It's time to move. Lolena, sweetheart, it's time for you to go," Hercules instructed. The two went out the back; Hercules lifted her over her fence; her neighbor helped her down; she went over the next neighbor's fence and that neighbor helped her down. She walked up the street and got into the SUV that was waiting for her. "Looks like we're saving you again. Two days in a row, that's a record," teased Nathaniel and he drove Lolena to Hercules's house; he texted Hercules: I got the package.

Hercules looked at the group standing in the living room ready for the next set of instructions, "Alvin, your mother is on her way, now are you all ready? Remember, no talking, no looking around, just move straight to the limo." Hercules turned all the lights out, checked all the doors and windows, set the alarm, "Let's go." Two group members were in front, Ivan and Pookie; Alvin and Josh took decoy

Lolena (Sheila) by the arm, they were in the middle and Carl and Nupe brought up the rear; they walked swiftly to the limo. There was so many cameras flashing you would have thought Beyoncé was getting into the limo. Hercules shut the front door, stood on the porch, looked all around, walked to the limo and got in. "Didn't we do this yesterday?" Rafeki said as he drove off.

The limo headed to the Silverstone Bay Executive Suite Inn; the 300 air-conditioned guestrooms located by the waterfront features coffee/tea makers and complimentary weekday newspapers and internet connection. Refrigerators and microwaves are offered. Bathrooms feature shower/tub combinations and hair dryers. In addition to desks, guestrooms offer phones with voice mail, as well as free local calls, LCD televisions have premium cable channels, video-game consoles, and pay movies. Also included are windows that open and blackout drapes/curtains. Housekeeping is offered daily, and guests may request wake-up calls. Hercules made arrangements to accommodate the Lolena Wynn decoy crew in the pen house suite. Rafeki drove up the driveway, the decoy crew quickly exited the limo, per instructions they went straight to the elevator, top floor, and key card into the room. "Now this is what I'm talking about," said Alvin as he and the crew looked around the presidential suite, which offered a few more amenities and had a spectacular view. "No problem, we can hang out here for a couple of weeks and report wherever we are needed, Hercules." "Let's not get too excited. I don't want you guys pulling a Charlie Sheen or M.C. Hammer to this room. Remember the rules ladies and gentlemen, do not go anywhere in the Inn; you may order room service; do not talk to anyone. Tonight all of you stay here, we will rotate schedules as the days go by; we need to convince the media mob that Lolena will be staying here, and this is the best way to keep her safe. However, it looks like the population of Silverstone Bay increased by twenty thousand these past few days, and a good portion of them seem to be staying here so, I reiterate, do not go out these doors unless one of the Brothas is with you. Does everyone understand, this is extremely critical, and I hate to say it, but things are still very dangerous right now; Silverstone Bay is still under attack." "Are you going to keep my mother safe?" Alvin asked with concern. Hercules walked over to Alvin, stood in front of him, looked him in his eyes and said, "You have asked me twice what my intentions are with your mother. I want to let you know right here in front of your friends and God, I will lay my life down before I let anything happen to her!" Alvin embraced him and said, "Give her a kiss for me."

****

Nathaniel escorted her in, showed her where everything was located to help her make herself feel at home until he got there. After he secured the place, he left, and she poured herself a glass of wine and took the alone time to begin her research on the duties and responsibilities of a mayor. Lolena was in front of Hercules' computer in his study. It had been just forty-eight hours since the citizens of Silverstone Bay self-elected her to fill the now vacant mayor seat. Before that moment, she had never given any thought to being a mayor, a councilperson, a board member, class president, cheerleader, nothing in that capacity that required a voting constituent to vote her into the position. She remembered years ago in high school, she was nominated for homecoming queen, she had to participate in all the homecoming events and the student body conducted the secret ballot, and when the announcement was made at the

73

homecoming game, she didn't win, and Lolena remembered how disappointed she felt; she secretly cried in the bathroom. Since Lolena decided to run based on being nominated by the voting constituents of Silverstone Bay, deep inside, she wanted to win.

"Lena do your due diligence and learn all you can about becoming the next mayor of Silverstone Bay," she said to herself aloud. "Well, I see you are making yourself at home," the deep voice came from behind her.

"Well, hello handsome," Lolena turned around in her chair. "Your place is pretty nice. These old Victorian homes have so much character, but once you step inside here, you would think you were in a high-tech home from some futuristic galaxy. Looks like you like the same afro-centric décor I love. Your renovations are coming along nicely," she complimented. "Thank you. I have wanted to have you over for some time, but I didn't think it would be under these circumstances. It has been a very, very interesting forty-eight hours; but before you get too deep into your research, you need to get a good night's rest. This will be my last directive to you today, step away from the computer, come with me and I will show you to your room." Hercules stood

74

there, held out his hand, she stood up, strolled to him, took his hand, and they went upstairs.

Monday Morning

Lolena opened her eyes; slid up, stretched, yawned, and looked around the room admiring the orderly layout of the cozy room. She looked herself as she sat in bed, in the mirror of the old-fashioned styled walnut mirror/dresser that sat between the two tall, four by six, white double-pane windows with light green, bespoke shutters; the textured wall treatment imaged golden-wood panels; the floor treatment was a plush, dark green carpet. There was a beautiful old-fashion styled wardrobe closet on the left side of the room; the bathroom on the right side; she could see the vessel sink vanity. It felt like she slept on a cloud, the bed mattress was soft but firm, the sheets were green, probably 1000 thread count and smelled like butter-cream vanilla candy, but the smell of coffee and bacon, quickly, consumed her nose after she heard the knock at the door, "Come in" she said, and Hercules opened the door. It smelled delicious, but he looked delicious standing there wearing black slacks, starched, light-green shirt and a black and green silk tie, his shoes were smooth and shining. She looked down at herself and didn't recognize the large t-shirt she was wearing.

"Good morning, beautiful, I hope you slept well. You practically were sleeping before your head hit the pillow. We were talking; you said I am so tired and laid your head down. I hope you don't mind, but I wanted you to be comfortable, so I put one of my t-shirts on you; I tried not to look as I disrobed you. You were so tired, the events of the past few days must have hit you all at that moment; anyways, you needed your rest because, baby, you/we have things to do. You still want to be mayor of Silverstone Bay? You saw how crowds are attracted to you now. How does that feel? I know how I feel. I don't want to sound worried, but we must organize all activities from now until you get elected mayor of Silverstone Bay," he smiled and sat on the bed next to her. She leaned on his left shoulder.

"Well first of all, I slept like a baby. What time is it? I have to get to work," she said as she started to look around for her phone. "Don't worry about the time right now; I let you sleep in; again, because you need all the rest you can get. The days will be long from this point forward. We have a campaign to run." Lolena turned to look at her hero, "You got that right because I'm going to be the next mayor of Silverstone Bay. I'm goin' to own the position right here, right now. You, me, my son, the people are going to make that happen. We're ready!" She, instinctively, hugged him; he hugged her back. "Well, here we are again, in bed, weren't we in bed like this yesterday?" She said bashfully. She felt her nipples get hard and felt a smooth twinge between her legs. Hercules pulled back and looked her straight in the eyes, he moved his hand gently across her face; he glided is hand down to her breast and cupped it and felt her hard nipple; he stopped and stood up.

Lolena looked at him but didn't say a word. He spoke, "Please excuse my forwardness; I don't want you to feel I am taking advantage of you. Don't get me wrong, I want you, I want you real bad. I'm sure I'd scare you if I told you exactly how bad I want you. I have thought about making love to you since the first time we danced at Dominic's a few months ago; when I finally got to kiss you, well you were there, you felt it; it felt good, you felt good, you feel good right now, but I want to make love to you under a less stressful situation. Right now, I am serious as a heart attack; if anything were to happen to you now that you are in the spotlight, I wouldn't be able to live another day. I made a promise to your son that I would take care of you even if my life depended on it. I meant it. So, sweetheart, this moment isn't our moment; our moment will come, believe me; so be ready for it. Now, like I just said, let's get ready for this campaign. Ok? Does that sound ok with you? Hercules says with sincerity. Lolena didn't say another word. She stood up, took his arms wrapped them around her now naked body, she let him squeeze her ass, caress her breast, kiss her gently on the lips, stepped back and said, "I just

79

wanted you to feel what you have to keep safe," and walked in the bathroom, shutting the door behind her. Hercules composed himself and spoke as best he could, "Breakfast is ready and I will meet you downstairs," and quickly left the room.

****

Lolena dressed as if she were going into the office, black slacks, cream colored, silk, tank top, short, black and white houndstooth jacket, pearl jewelry, black stilettos. She pulled some of her locs up and wrapped them in a red and black scarf, her makeup was flawless. She admired herself in the mirror; said a prayer; and said to herself "Lena, it's on, feet don't fell me now," and joined Hercules, downstairs, for breakfast.

"I'm famished; it smells so good," Lolena says as she entered the kitchen. Hercules had everything sat out on the island, turkey bacon, hash browns, scrambled eggs, fruit, wheat toast and fresh-squeezed orange juice. His kitchen was very chic. The smooth, black cabinetry and silver stainless steel appliances lined the sixteen by sixteen, hardwood-floored kitchen that was illuminated by fluorescent lighting from the Minka Lavery style ceiling fixture and sunlight from the duke stone castle styled windows; the tiled, white-stoned wall treatment blended the kitchen so eloquently. The couple ate in silence but glanced at each other through sensuous eyes the entire meal. Hercules brought them back to the moment, "I'm going to work, you're safe here, I guarantee that, feel free to go anywhere in the house, my house is now your house, but do not go outside any of these doors. Are we clear on that?" "Today, I am going to learn all what it takes to be a mayor. I'm going back into the study and resume my research. You're going to go check on my son and his crew before you go in, aren't you?" she said. "Of course, I will call you. I'll be back before you know it," he kisses her passionately and quickly leaves.

****

Lolena types google.com in the web browser; then types: responsibilities of a city mayor into Google's textbox and selects the first option and reads:

As the head of the city, mayors have several roles. They must represent the city in front of state legislatures, federal agencies and other government officials. They also meet and greet important visitors to the city and their own constituents; mayors also

81

have a duty to participate in ceremonial activities, including dedications and other public events.

Mayors preside over city council meetings and in some cities mayors may vote as a council member. As the presiding officer, the mayor calls the meeting to order, recognizes speakers and ensures that the meeting's agenda is followed. In some cities, mayors create committees and appoint members to committees that advise the city council.

Mayors carry out the laws passed by the legislature in their city. Mayors work with the city council and other departments of the local government to enact legislation. Depending on the city's form of government, mayors may have the power to veto any ordinance passed by the city council. The mayor signs any legislation passed and all other official documents.

Mayors propose and approve the annual budget for their city. They must also oversee the appropriation of funds to city agencies and departments. The mayor, as well as the city council, works to recruit new business to increase the revenue of the city and to create new jobs.

"I can do this; I do this all day as Executive Director of the training center; running a non-profit is like being mayor, 'a mayor of the non-profit'; both require diplomacy. I know as clear as I'm sitting here, I can do a better job than what Mayor Burton has done the past two years," she says to herself. She further researches the responsibilities of the city manager and council since they will be the people that will have to work with her. "Well, I deem myself qualified for the mayor position; now let me call my office to see what's going on."

****

Sherwood walks into Hercules' office and greets him, "How's it hanging?" "It's hanging very well, thank you for asking," Hercules replies. "Have you given any thought to how you will run the department now that Jackass Jennings is behind bars?" Sherwood asked.

It just dawned on Hercules that he was now the Interim Chief of Police of Silverstone Bay police department. "Lolena is now running for mayor, if, I mean when she wins, she will be on the committee to appoint the next chief of police; this could be a serious conflict of interest because I plan on asking her to marry me," he said. "Marry?" Sherwood asked, "Did I hear you say marry?"

Press Conference

Thursday morning started quiet in comparison to the loud press-conference prep session held at Hercules's house the night before. Lolena worked late into the night on her speech along with Hercules as her sounding board. Alvin and his crew including Sheila (Alvin's new girlfriend), the Band of Brothas wives and significant others, Zelma (Smokey Mike's wife), Stephanie (Sherwood's wife), Kena (Rafeki's girlfriend), Stacy (Sonnie's wife), Andrea (Nathaniel's wife) role-played as the discourteous media and unruly crowd, and the Band of Brothas strategized the security detail. Lolena awoke at 5:30 a.m., she listened to the silence of the morning and announced, "I'm ready!" then put it in gear. She did her morning exercise routine using Hercules' state-of-the-art workout equipment stationed in his garage; a half hour on the Bowflex treadclimber gave her ample cardio, two hundred reverse crunches, side-to-side twists and floor bicycling helped her fight the battle of the bulge and twenty-five push-ups and pull-ups allowed her to compete with arms like First Lady Michelle Obama.

"Why didn't you wake me, I'd have come out here with you," Hercules said as he walked behind her and massaged her shoulders while she was sitting on the bench drinking some water. "I didn't want to bother you, we were up so late, and for some reason I was wide awake at five-thirty. If we were on a farm, I'm sure I would've beaten the chickens walking up," she giggles at her little joke. "My father used to call me his little chicken when I was a little girl. He would be so proud of me now," she thinks about him for a second, "So today; I'm going to make him proud. I'm not sure how everything is going to go today, but I don't have any expectation, so everything is good; well, don't 'cha think?" "Baby, I have no doubts that you will razzle dazzle the crowd, remember they are the ones who

put you here. You just have to tell them to get
everyone they know out to vote, and like they said,
"Lolena Wynn, write her in!"

****

Jennifer Jason and Mr. G went over the
details of the day's plot. "We don't want to stick out
in the crowd. We need to blend in as Lolena Wynn
supporters, but that might be hard because she has so
many nigger supporters, a white man and a Spanish
woman could be suspicious; you saw the way those
people looked us at that RapCity club," he said with a
stench of paranoia on each word. "Those people
weren't staring at us, they were staring at me; I was
gorgeous in the stunning red dress. They were
practically begging to kiss the bottom of my shoes if
I would have let any of them get close to me," she
said like the conceited bitch she is. "Wear the beige
polyester pants with the beige polo shirt and brown
penny loafers; those fancy tailored cut suits you look
so good in will draw too much attention. Before you
put on your pants, let me…," she walked over to him,
got down on her knees, took his cock in her mouth
and sucked real hard in an in and out motion. "Um,
um, um give it to me, give it to me...Ummm, Ummm,
you're so hard you fuckin' stallion, I feel it coming,

86

come on, give it to ME!" She said, and she suck hard and fast on his hard dick. "Yeah, that's it, here it comes," and he yanked his dick out of her mouth and came all over her face; she licked it up like a melting ice-cream cone on a hot summer day.

Mr. G squeezed the last bit of his come out, grabbed her by the back of her neck and hair, yanked her to her feet and said, "Don't think your shit don't stink, you sadistic bitch; don't fuck up today! Get the shots we need so you can send Miss Lolena those pictures that will make her head spin. She thinks she's going to take the mayor position, she has another thing coming. The backup plan to get the city manager in the mayor's seat is part of the plan now. She and mayor Burton have been having an affair for some time, she knows what to do."

****

Margaret Toolly had been the Silverstone Bay city manager for two years, before that she was an administrative clerk for the city for seven years. She and Mayor Burton started having an affair a couple years ago; many suspected something was going on when she became the city manager when he was re-elected. When she was an administrative clerk, she wore a meek, mild demeanor around the office; when she became city manager, the dresses got shorter, the blouses got tighter, the shoe heels got taller; the hair color went from dull brown to sassy red and her attitude changed just as dramatic as her attire.

Margaret sat alone in the mayor's office; she knew if anything were to happen to the mayor, she was to go to his office, clear out all files, documents, and any incriminating evidence that would expose more dirt then what was already spilled. They had discussed the possibility of her stepping into the mayor position if things went in the wrong direction; well things did go in the wrong direction according to the plan. Now she could show them all, she has what it takes; she was no longer the homely little girl nobody wanted to play with; she was going to be the next mayor of Silverstone Bay.

"Lolena Wynn you think you are going to be the next mayor, ha ha ha, I hope you won't be too upset when I upstage you at the press conference. Yeah, the mayor and chief of police are now behind bars because they were so stupid to be caught on tape blabbing to the world the plans to bring a private prison complex to the old military base. The people of Silverstone Bay are going to be surprised that it will actually happen; the papers have been signed," she busted at the seam laughing, sitting in the mayor's office, all by herself.

****

It was a bright, sunny day. There was not a cloud in the sky. The maintenance crew was setting up the city center plaza. The event planner was walking around handing out instructions. The plaza was politically decorated with red, white and blue streamers and balloons. The stage area was set up with chairs, a podium and a sound system. Since media crews, both national and international besieged Silverstone Bay, the entire west side of city hall was sectioned off to accommodate the capacity.

The events of Silverstone Bay turned the Jewel by the Bay into the most attractive city to visit and/or live. The population grew overnight; local realtors had never been so busy; city departments were inundated with permit requests for business, construction, pets, parking; school enrollments tripled; grocery stores had to double shipments, retail outlets saw a significant increase in sales at all levels. As with all political elections, the paraphernalia shops sprung up overnight; all over the city; Lolena Wynn t-shirts were the main seller; the shirts came in all colors with the slogan: Lolena Wynn Write Her In.

The politically converted tour bus, which had all the amenities a traveling politician would need, was stationed in the private parking lot in the back of city hall; the Lolena Wynn campaign crew, everyone wearing, in some form, the colors red, white and blue, sat ready and waiting. "We expected lots of people, but more than that decided to come," Hercules said as he observed the crowd swelling by the minute. "Sherwood is positioned in the security command trailer; he'd arranged for as much security as the city could contract; the mayor of San Francisco was very helpful in lending Silverstone Bay the use of its security teams; they are very use to large crowds. Rafeki and Smokey Mike are posted across the street on the top floor of the building right across from where you will be standing when you give your acceptance speech. Alvin, you will stand on the left side of your mother, I will be on the right. Nathanial and Sonnie, stand on both side of the ladies behind us; J-Knock crew, stand on both sides of them. I want everyone to stand tall and proud, keep your eyes open and alert. There are many people out there, and not all of them love Lolena. Are there any questions?" Hercules stood tall as he looked at the people ready to go to do what they rehearsed. "I have a question," Lolena said. "Yes, Ms. Wynn," Hercules said with authority. "Are you ready?" she said with sass in her voice. He walked over to her, cupped her face in his hands, and kissed her for exactly one minute, "Now, I'm ready."

Lolena stood in front of the crowd; there were people as far as she could see; she marveled at all the banners, flags, streamers, and balloons flying about. The crowd clapped for ten minutes straight; tears welled up in her eyes; she looked at her son standing there, tears were in his eyes. When she looked at Hercules, he was staring at her as if magnet were drawing him closer; he wasn't smiling; his eyes just pierced her soul.

"Ladies and Gentlemen, I accept your self-elected nomination to be the next Mayor of Silverstone Bay!" and that's all she had to say; the crowd didn't need to hear another word, she was their candidate; the ovation lasted for twenty minutes; the chant started again: "Lolena Wynn Write Her In!"

The crowd settled down. Margaret Toolly came over to Lolena; she recognized her as the city manager. "Excuse me, but I would like to say something as a city official," she said with a non-threatening smile and gave Lolena a hug. She began to speak, "I would like to say a few words as a city representative of the beautiful city of Silverstone Bay. I am the city manager, and as the city manager I want to see this fair city regain its leadership, therefore, I, Margaret Toolly will be a write-in candidate for mayor of Silverstone Bay." The crowd erupted. Mr. G and Jennifer Jason were in the crowd; she took continuous shots from the Canon zoom lens camera of Hercules and Lolena.

Campaign Headquarters – RapCity

The 51st Street RapCity Club owned and operated by Rap Legend Peace B Out; he had earned ten Grammies over his fifteen-year career. He lets local talents use his club to write their songs and produce music videos; every Friday is local talent night and one local talent artist is given exclusive rights for the entertainment that night; the artist can perform live, their videos are shown, and the only music played that night is their music.

Peace B Out earned his Grammies rapping very explicit, degrading, demoralizing, graphic, violent music, if you want to call it music, and videos; there was so much obscene language that most of the songs couldn't be played on mainstream radio and the ones that did, had so many bleeps it seemed pointless to attempt to listen to, let alone dance. Depending on whom you talked to, either you loved his brand of music or hated it. He was not on an island alone. The rap music industry turned into a billion dollar industry; where there was that quantity of dollars the vultures, pit bulls, lions, tigers of greed came; but this is no news bulletin; mostly everyone did what they did for the money. Peace didn't consider himself a greedy man; he earned his money the honest way, yes it came from production of Gangsta rap; but he turned around and did what he could to help the next up-and-coming rap artist. However, recently his outlook on the business changed.

Rafeki Soladad met Peace B Out a few years ago; he had come into the bank, Silverstone Bay Bank, where Rafeki worked as the branch manager; he opened an account with a sizable deposit, so Rafeki took the time to meet with Peace B Out to discuss his goals and objectives. He admired the success of Peace and personality wise the two men connected; even though Rafeki would never buy a rap record, he admired Peace' business sense, cool personality, and his intelligence.

One day at a lunch meeting, Rafeki shared with Peace an internet article outlining the systematic approach some un-named music industry executive devised years ago to change the rap game; they wanted rap artist to go Gangsta rap and they threw millions of dollars into promoting and distributing Gangsta rap. Artist who came to them with socially conscious rap music were un-promoted by the big dogs. The reason for the heavy promotion of Gangsta rap was part of a bigger picture: the private prison industrial complex. Gangsta rap was used to promote aggressive behavior, which, resulted in criminal behavior, which, resulted in prison sentences, which, resulted in housing the inmates at one of the private prisons. Private prisons are owned by shareholders who are looking for profits for every prisoner who is sentenced at one of these facilities. The government is paying the corporations who own these prisons; it is extremely profitable to keep the prisons booked at full capacity. "Private prisons are a billion dollar industry. The corporations and the people who own these corporations are well known: national banks, politicians, wealthy individuals. The projected

95

growth of the private prisons is staggering; the system is worried that the crime rate is going down, so corporations are lobbying for longer sentencing, i.e. the three-strike law; delaying decisions on immigrants thus holding them behind bars longer. Years ago, the big music exec wanted to use Gangsta rap as a vehicle to send our people to one of those filthy institutions; modern-day slavery is alive and growing," Rafeki said with sad anger in his voice. "I feel bad. I mean I know there's a lot bullshit out there that will keep a brotha down, but I really don't want to be a contributing factor to that process," said Peace.

Peace B Out made the decision to turn RapCity into the Lolena Wynn Campaign headquarters for the next three weeks. When the video went viral of Jackass Jennings and Mayor Burton plotting to turn the old military base into a private prison industrial complex, he said to himself, "if there is anything I can do to stop that bullshit, count me in." What better way for him to own up to his own words than to have the campaign headquarters right there in the club. RapCity is known for its promotion of rap artists. "I'll be dam if any artists that come out my establishment contributes one penny to anyone's private prison!" he confirms his commitment to that cause.

The Lolena Wynn campaign crew convened in the upstairs VIP sectioned of the club. Alvin and the J-Knock Ent. members laughed out loud as they sat at the tables which replaced the usual VIP red-velvet cushion lounge seating, "Man, we were just up here doing some crazy stuff before and now look at us, campaigning." "Sweetheart, thank you, thank all of you. This means so much to me. You guys are still cool, don't worry, you will still be cool after campaigning, look at President Obama," Lolena said and gave her son a fist bump.

"We're not going to meet long," she began, "Today was our first day of official campaigning. We only have three weeks and those three will fly by. If we're lucky, we might get some sleep but don't count on it. We don't know how this race is going to turn out; it's the first time its ever happened this way. In all my years of voting, the candidate I chose was on the ballot. I guess the main thing we have to communicate is how to complete the ballot. We can send out sample ballots illustrating how a person should complete a ballot when you write in the candidate of your choice. There really isn't much time to do the entire campaign activities required, but we will do as much as we can. Now that we see we have an opponent, do you think it will turn into an ugly campaign?" In unison, the campaign crew said, "YES!"

****

Jennifer uploaded the pictures she took at the press conference to the HP laptop; she shot one thousand pictures; the continuous-shot mode allows for hundreds of shots in a matter of minutes. She previewed all the shots from the second Hercules and Lolena she dubbed 'peasant woman' walked onto the stage. She spent hours reviewing each shot; she selected a few shots that she felt she could manipulate, in Photoshop, to paint a destructive picture for the peasant woman and trap Hercules into her twisted web of hatred. "You'll regret the day you rejected me, Hercules. What will your peasant woman say about your bastard boy you abandoned? She won't think you are so wonderful after she sees these pictures," she says with so much jealousy she almost choked on her words.

"Come here," commanded Mr. G. She got up, walked over to him where he was sitting back in the chair; he looked at her, took a swig from the bottle of beer, unzipped his pants, pulled out his cock, she got down on her knees and instinctively sucked his dick. He pulled her head back, stood her up, turned her around and entered from behind. She held onto the chair as he pounded her hard, he suddenly stopped, she turned around quickly, she wanted more, "now get down here and suck my come out, I know you want it," he commanded. She finished sucking him and resumed her Photoshop project.

Margaret's Campaign

Margaret met Mr. G and Jennifer in the restaurant out on the patio at the Fairmount Inn for breakfast the day after the press conference. There was not much conversation during breakfast; Margaret, wearing a tailored royal blue business suit, placed her order with the hostess, "One egg over easy, glass of grapefruit juice and a bowl of fruit, please." Mr. G, wearing a dark Armani suit, blue silk shirt, white silk tie, ordered, "five slices of bacon, three sausages, scrambled eggs, hash brown, toast and a glass of milk," and Jennifer, wearing a tight, bright green, sleeveless cotton dress, matching jewelry, shoes, purse and shades ordered, " a Spanish omelet, please."

"That went well, yesterday," said Mr. G. "Yes, it did," said Margaret. "Lolena Wynn was completely caught off guard, and that was just the beginning of the end of her campaign. The audacity of her and that crowd to think she could ever be mayor of Silverstone Bay," she sipped her coffee and continued spewing. "I have the files from John's office tucked away at my place; his computer data was backed up and hard drive erased. I was able to get all that out before the Feds came and seized just about everything in his office. Do you have the package?" "Not so fast," said Mr. G. "Don't you have a package for me?" "Yes, here it is," and she removed an envelope out of her briefcase and slid it over to him. He reached for the envelope and touched the top of her hand and held it for a few seconds and looked at her; then took the envelope and put it in his inside pocket of his jacket. Jennifer peeped the document exchange and shot a sideways glance at Margaret; she darted a look back at Jennifer and then asked, "where's my package?" Mr. G took an envelope out of his other pocket, handed it to her, and said, "This should take care of everything you need to win the campaign."

Jennifer wiped her mouth with the napkin; sat it back on her lap; she cleared her throat, scooted in closer to the table, "how do we know you won't fuck this up? How do we know you didn't set the mayor up to take the fall? It seems pretty convenient for you to walk into the mayor's seat. The operation lost some good men behind the Code Black fiasco, one of them my husband," sneered Jennifer. "You think I had something to do with that falling apart," Margaret snapped; "From what I see, you don't look much like a grieving widow. Your husband's body is still at the morgue." "Don't worry about how I look, you fuck this up, you will be joining my husband's body at the morgue," she said between gritted teeth. Mr. G intercepted the two feuding women, "It's not time for a cat fight right now. Swallow that bullshit right now and let's deal with what needs to be done. In three weeks, we need to have everything in place to pull off the Code Red plan. Margaret, run the campaign according to the script; schedule a few TV interviews; run ads in the local newspaper; make sure your opponent agrees to one debate. We need to inundate Silverstone Bay with as much bad press as possible about Lolena Wynn. Does anybody here have a problem with the plan?"

****

Margaret purchased a series of ads with the Silverstone Bay Post: Lolena - Is She Qualified?; Lolena Wynn is Not a Resident of Silverstone Bay; Lolena Wynn – Where Are Your College Transcripts?; Lolena Wynn's Son has Affiliation with Local Gangs; Young Lolena Wynn Found in a Drunken Stupor After Wild Night Out.

Next, Margaret scheduled a series of television interviews; she took advantage of all the media coverage that the mayoral election has drawn both locally and nationally; scheduling an interview proved to be extremely easy.

"Hello, this is Chisti Barber of Channel Five news and today we have in our station one of the candidates running for the vacant mayor seat, Margaret Toolly. Good Evening Margaret, thank you for taking the time out of your busy campaigning schedule to talk to us about how you think the campaign is going."

"Thank you Chisti for the opportunity to speak with you and to my constituents here in Silverstone Bay. First, I want to thank everyone for your kind words and all the support you have shown me. You can understand how difficult it is working to keep the city running and conduct a campaign in such a short time frame. However, the love and support I am getting is showing up in the polls. I mean, I don't get all caught up in the numbers, but the polls show my campaign is gaining points by the day." "Really? How are you managing to keep it all together?"

"We put a top-notch campaign crew together. We have been working non-stop ever since I put my name in the hat. We are confident that we will win. I don't want to give too much credence to anything that is said about my opponent but I privy to some information which is highly damaging to my opponent. As a voter myself, I would question some of the things that are reported in the news. I wouldn't want in office a person with loose morals and raising a child with gang affiliations. Furthermore, being qualified for the position is extremely vital. I mean, what are her qualifications? What, she some kind of community organizer and that makes her qualified? From what I hear, she just moved to Silverstone Bay two months ago. I'm just saying, as a concerned citizen of this fair city, I am the candidate for Mayor."

"Well, Ok, I see you have given us a lot to think about, but before we go, you do know that the current President of the United States of America was a community organizer. I'm just saying. This is Chisti Barber and we have just concluded the one and only television interview with Margaret Toolly, a write-in candidate for mayor. Wait a minute…what was that…really, really, ok, ok…Excuse me TV audience, I just received word that the Lolena Wynn Campaign just called the station and said that there will be a debate the day before Election Day. They said that Lolena will be there and if anybody else wants to join her, she will be on the front steps of city hall where she accepted her nomination to be the next mayor of Silverstone Bay. There you have it; this is Chisti Barber signing off and we will see you at the debates if not before, Good Evening."

****

Margaret felt she had done an excellent job of smoke screening the people into thinking she had a large campaign crew. In reality, it was just her and her ability to pay people off. So far, all she had done was buy airtime and ads in newspapers, but studies showed that those forms of media could be remarkably effective. "These people of Silverstone

105

Bay are just stupid, you can tell them anything, they will believe it," she thought to herself as she sat alone in her apartment. There was a knock at her door, she peeked through the peephole and opened the door. Mr. G walked in. She walked to her bedroom, and he followed her. She disrobed and laid on her bed. Mr. G took off his clothing, placed everything neatly on the chair. He handed her a condom, and she put it on him. He got on top of her, spread her legs, rammed his cock inside her and pumped hard, he stopped, stood up, took off the condom, "here finish me off." She sat up on her knees and sucked him until he pulled out and came on her. He dressed and left.

Win With Wynn Campaign Fundraiser Event

Five days before the debate, the Lolena Wynn's campaign prepared for the evening's fundraiser event at RapCity, busy campaign headquarters by day, by night, a hip-hop club filled with partygoers. During this short election period, patrons of all ages partied at RapCity; the genre of music expanded from just hip hop to R&B, oldies, jazz, country, pop, new age; even though the watered-down versions of hip hop dominated. Peace B Out donated all nightclub activities proceeds towards the campaign: instructional pamphlets on completing write-in ballots; locations of voting polls;

detailed informational brochures about Lolena Wynn – her biography, platform and beliefs.

"I'm just not going to stoop to the level of my opponent and play dirty politics, said Lolena; "There is just not enough time, and I seriously don't want to waste time on blatant lies." "I agree, said Zelma. "Second that." said Andrea. "There are just five days before Election Day and absolutely every minute counts so let's finish this final mailing, get ready for the interview, make sure all details are checked off for tonight's party," Lolena concluded. "Tonight's guest list is star studded," said Stacy, "it looks like a who's who of the Bay Area. All advanced tickets have been sold, there are still tickets allocated for sale at the door tonight, but it looks like those will go quickly; there's a line forming outside already," reported Stephanie. "The entertainment is here and rehearsing in the studios. "Looks like your son is on the program. Have you ever heard your son perform, Lena?" asked Kena. "Well, not really because I really don't care for hip-hop, well Gangsta rap. I used to burn up the dance floor off Sugar Hill Gang Rapper's Delight song you know back in the day of clean rap. I hear Alvin in his room with his crew rehearsing, but I only tolerate very little of that, so I holler at them to turn the noise down," said Lolena. The women reminisced a few minutes.

The crowds were too large anywhere Lolena went, so she only conducted interviews at RapCity. Today she granted a short interview with the local reporter Chisti Barber. Lolena knew to be careful in speaking with her; she remembered her last encounter with the reporter the way she tended to put words in her mouth; Hercules convinced her to grant the interview because this reporter had helped him in the past with some very useful information; Lolena conceited to a very short interview. A campaign worker came and informed her, the reporter was downstairs. Lolena checked herself in the mirror on the wall and went down to get the interview over.

"Hello Ms. Barber, looks like you have your crew ready to go, I'm ready so let's get started," Lolena said as she shook the reporter's hand. "Thank you, Ms. Wynn, I appreciate your time. It wasn't that easy to schedule an interview, with all the media attention this campaign is generating, so I won't take up much of your time. "So Ms. Wynn it is truly a phenomenal how you were nominated by the people of Silverstone Bay. With the shameful way, the former mayor and chief of police got caught participating in criminal activity that practically ran the city into the ground, how are you going to fix the problems? Your opponent has questioned your experience, the gang involvement of your son, your residency, your moral behavior and your level of education; do you have a response for those acquisitions? What can you say to the people of Silverstone Bay on why they should trust you as mayor? Lolena looked at Chisti straight in the eye, and then she turned to the camera and said, "Well, Chisti, most of your questions you asked require an answer because the people of Silverstone Bay want to know what is going to happen now. They want to know why they should trust me as their mayor. As far as what my opponent is saying, she can ask me those questions at the debate. I said I would be in front of City Hall the day before Election Day if she wants to ask me those questions, she'd better show up, five o'clock, on the stairs of city hall. The people of Silverstone Bay have had my back since the beginning; I'm going to take this opportunity, in front of the camera, and say to all of you who are watching, "I got 'cha your Back. So, if I don't talk to you again before Election Day, remember to go vote and let's Win With Wynn!" and Lolena concludes

110

the interview with a shimmy shake and a "Woo Who" to the camera.

****

The doors opened, at five thirty, to begin letting the guests and supporters into RapCity for the fundraising event. The guest list was a Who's Who of celebrities and political figures: Former San Francisco Mayors Willie Brown and Gavin Newsom, Congresswoman Barbara Lee, Political Activist, Scholar, and Author Angela Davis, Political Activist, Actor and Film Director Danny Glover, Green Jobs Guru and former White House Green Jobs Adviser Van Jones and more.

Lolena, the Band of Brothas, and Peace B Out were in a back studio where they were conducting a video conference with Michelle Alexander, author of The New Jim Crow and weekend talk show host of MSNBC Melissa Perry-Harris. "Hello ladies, it's good to see you again so soon after our last meeting. Thank you for taking the time out of your busy schedules to meet the next mayor of Silverstone Bay, Lolena Wynn," Hercules spoke to the ladies on the video monitor and pulled Lolena closer to him and gave her a squeeze hug. "Hello Ms. Alexander, it is a divine pleasure to meet you. I want to extend a personal invitation to come to Silverstone Bay and speak with the people here. Your book is so on point with what some people tried to do here. How soon can you get here?" Lolena asks. "Call me Michelle; it is a true pleasure to meet you. Hercules shared with us how you rose up from the people as their self-appointed leader. From what I see on this monitor, they knew what they were doing putting you in charge. As soon as you want to send me the invitation, I'll be there. The bay area is a beautiful part of the country, and Silverstone Bay is a place I now need to visit. Good Luck on the election. I know the next time I speak to you, it will be Mayor Lolena Wynn," said Michelle. "Melissa Perry, I watch your show as often as I can. It's a pleasure to you and to my surprise, we're sorors," beamed Lolena. "You mean to tell me the next mayor of Silverstone Bay is a member of Delta Sigma Theta! I'm going to have to have you come on my show. Soon after you get settled in your new position, we will make that happen. Good Luck, my sista," said Melissa. "Don't mean to end the conversation so soon, but we all have to get back to campaigning. The event downstairs has started already. Alright ladies, we're still here for you, until the next time, continue to do all the great things you do," said Hercules. "This was a highlight for me to meet such dynamite women. We will stay in touch," Lolena said as the monitor faded to black. "Ain't this about a bitc...," Peace B Out stopped before completing that word, "Look who walked in the Club?"

****

RapCity was packed; there was no more room for anyone in the building; an erected large canopy tent, sat up in the back of the club, accommodated the overflow. Along with the regular chef at RapCity, Chef Pat who was frying fish like that was the last fish in the sea, contracted local restaurants assisted in serving the unusually large crowd of Lolena Wynn supporters. A favorite local restaurant of the Band of Brothas', Mac-Cee's, brought their famous Philly cheese sandwiches. Event guests feasted on other tasty items: broiled/baked/fried or BBQ chicken, mac and cheese, collards, salads, fruit, snacks, and desserts. There was a beverage selection from water to whiskey. Along with food and drink, there was plenty of entertainment.

Stephanie took the microphone and made an announcement, "Can I get the next mayor of

Silverstone Bay to come to the stage?" The crowd clapped and cheered; Lolena came to the stage. She wore a campaign T-shirt with the slogan 'Win With Wynn' and white stretch pants and red stilettos. More cheering and clapping went on until she made it to the microphone. "We want to hear a few words from you before the next special entertainment performs," said Stephanie. "Is everybody having a good time! There's plenty to eat and drink so help yourself. Wow, so many people showed up tonight. I also see some famous faces in the mix. Thank you for all of your support. I know we have been campaigning for just a few weeks, but we've done a lot. The light is shining on this beautiful city of Silverstone Bay the Jewel by the Sea. Election Day will be in four days. If you haven't cast your early ballot, polls open seven a.m. So when you're completing your ballot, don't forget to slogan Lolena Wynn write her in!" Everyone claps and cheers.

"Ok, Lolena, your son, Alvin, some of you know him as Sixty B Mackin, would like to sing you a song," Stephanie said "Excuse me, did you say my son wants to sing me a song?" Lolena asked inquisitively. "Yes, Alvin and Sheila want to sing this song for you," she announced, "Ladies and Gentlemen, Alvin and Sheila."

"Mom, I love you, and I'm so proud of you," Alvin said and went over and kissed his mother on the cheek, Sheila kissed Lolena on the cheek. They stood in front of the mike and said, "We dedicate this song to you: You will Always Be the one for Me." The music started, and they sang in perfect pitch:

When I think of you and you think of me
We will always be free for thee
When I move along and I sing a song
You will Always Be the one for me

Now tha' the world sees all I've seen for so long
The world you See will always be the be the world
for me
So always be sure to run no more
You will Always Be the one for me

So baby, please, take stock in me
When your day seems so long
It won't be long, before you and me
Sing this song
You will Always Be the one for me
****

The Band of Brothas positioned strategically in proximity to the six-foot, three-inch, two hundred forty-five pounds, mocha-chocolate colored, broad shoulders man, wearing a short-waved style haircut,

115

dark suit, dark shades, and spit-shined shoes. He was a spitting image of Ball Player.

Surprises

The fundraiser was winding down even though there were several people still mingling. Hercules went up to the man who was a spitting image of Ball Player. The Ball Player Hercules knew should have been behind bars and for a long, long time. Could the man standing in RapCity at the fundraiser be the criminal Hercules himself took down? "Excuse me, sir we would like for you to come to the back with us," he asked with a 'don't give me a reason to knock you down right here' attitude.

The man looked at Hercules and went with him to the back. He led him to Peace B Out's office where Peace and the Brothas all gathered. "Please have a seat," Hercules instructed. "I'm not Ball Player," said Maurice after he sat down and looked at all the men in the room. Ricky Robinson was the identical twin of Marvin Robinson aka Ball Player, one of the members of the sinister group that came to Silverstone Bay with the pure intent to take it over by any means necessary. "Well, that was the million dollar question," said Sherwood, "Please go on." Ball Player is my twin brother. As you can see, we are identical twins. We may be identical in looks, but as God as my witness, that is where it stops." "If we didn't know your brother was behind bars right now, you certainly would have to prove you didn't escape from jail in some kind of miraculous feat. Even though I'm still going to check," said Sherwood. "I know, I get that all the time," said Maurice, "My knucklehead brother started getting into trouble when he was young, and on more than one occasion, I was the one who got the punishment. He wasn't as bad as he is now; things got bad for him when he got injured his second year in pro ball. I got tired of him and all his bullshit. I moved as far away from him as I could. So no one would mistake me for him. People are so gun crazy, they might have tried to take me out because of something he did thinking I'm him. I

118

didn't even tell him where I was. I felt it was better for my family and me; I'm married with two kids, one and two." "What are you doing here?" asked Hercules, "you see we thought you could have been him." "I know. You see, I know my brother is an idiot to the 'nth degree, but he's my brother. Our family is truly embarrassed that he was part of the cause of the some of the troubles in Silverstone Bay. I felt compelled to come here to see if I could do anything to help with the situation." There was silence in the room; breaking the silence Hercules said, "Maybe you can? Where are you staying?"

****

The Brothas met briefly to discuss details for the upcoming debate. Everyone had gone; the maintenance staff was cleaning, the women arrived to all their perspective homes safely. "So far, no crazy shit has happened," said Smokey Mike, "but I don't think we're in the clear." "We're not," said Sherwood. "I had the photo forensic department analyze the footage from the day Lolena accepted the nomination for mayor. There were so many people there, but a few stood out. Look up here on the monitor. These two people stuck out like a sore thumb. The woman wearing the overly tight dress and the man wearing the beige polyester pants with the beige polo shirt and brown penny loafers were such an odd couple. The woman continuously took pictures of you, Hercules and Lolena." Peace B Out walked into the office and saw the pictures displayed. "Hey, that's the guy that was here the other night with that woman. Man, that dress was so tight, I thought those titties were going to pop out onto the floor, and there would have been plenty of interested persons to pick them up. I also remember that guy from the time he was in here with Ball Player and a guy called Mr. E All those guys were a piece of work," informed Peace.

Hercules do you recognized the woman in the picture?" asked Sherwood, "she was relentless with her picture taking. You would have thought you were President Obama, and this was her opportunity to take as many pictures as she could possibly get." Hercules analyzed the pictures of the woman. Peace came back in with a disk, which he inserted in the video player, and the picture of the woman in the tight dress displayed in two-hundred zoom view. "She doesn't look like she changed much from college," Hercules said when he recognized the woman. "Yeah, that is her, big boobs and all. I want

120

to say her name is Jennifer. She was pretty hot back then. She screwed almost the entire football team. I passed on her when she came my way. I think I pissed her off. She thought everyone wanted her. If she is taking pictures of me now and that happened years ago, I would say she is still pissed. Let's keep our eyes on this couple. They are up to no good," Hercules determined.

"Hey Sonnie, what's going on with you? You're quieter than usual, asked Rafeki, "You still tripping about whatever your friend told you that day at the rodeo? What did she tell you?"

Sonnie sat in the chair with his chin resting on his knuckles, holding his drink in his other hand and contemplating if he should discuss what was on his mind. "Man, we have been so busy with the campaign that I realized I haven't been able to fathom what Tiffany told me. I was so shocked by it, I didn't see it coming." "Ok, what didn't you see coming?" asked Smokey Mike. "Well, she's going through some changes in her life, divorce, job and personal issues. Her personal issues involve her feelings for...," he pauses, finishes his drink, and looks at his brothas all looking at him. "Her feelings for you?" Sherwood asked. "No, her feelings for my

121

wife, Stacy," he said and fell back in the chair. "What!" all the brothas said in unison and burst out laughing.

****

Jennifer finished the Photoshop project and prepared the package for delivery. She just had to type up the letter for Lolena to read:

Dear Lolena, I'm writing you this letter as a highly-concerned citizen. You probably have looked at the pictures enclosed. I felt it was my civic duty to let you know with whom you are associating. Hercules McMarshall is not the person you think he is. He is heartless, abusive, a dead-beat dad, liar, cheater, manipulator, and untrustworthy. We met many years ago. He wanted to marry me. We had a baby out of wedlock. You see the resemblance. I moved to the area a few months ago, he found out where I lived, and he came over and forced himself upon me. I was afraid to go to the police because he is the police. When I saw that you are running for mayor, you are so beautiful, and I saw him standing next to you, I knew I had to speak out. You should know that man is an evil man. I will pray for you. Signed Concerned Citizen.

Jennifer sealed the envelope with a kiss. "We should go over the plan again. We can't afford any more fuck ups. I am concerned about if Margaret can do what she is supposed to do. She has to be in the right spot exactly at eight o'clock on Election Day. Did you get in contact with the guys with the big guns?" asked Jennifer as she looked at Mr. G lying on top of the bedspread fully dressed. He looked at her and said, "Come here." She walked over to him. "All we are going to do right now is make sure I am satisfied with you, take off your clothes and ride this stallion until I tell you to stop." She removed her clothes, and he removed his. He stroked himself while he watched her fondle herself. "I'm ready." She mounted him, slid her pussy onto his hard cock, and humped on top of him until he grabbed her to stop, pushed her back and sat up and jerked his come onto her naked body. "Everything is going to be in place for Code Red, just remember to write that second letter," he said and went to sleep.

Grandma

"Tell me about Grandma?" asked Donald as the Spencer family ate dinner. Family dinner is a wonderful experience in the Spencer home; they did not eat at the dinner table, not one time while Kayla was missing. Food was eaten elsewhere in the house: the living room, the bedroom, sitting at the counter in the kitchen. Life in the Spencer house was good. Donald moved his cousin, Phillip, into the spare room that was in the back of the house. It had a separate entrance into the house from outside; Phillip didn't have to come into the house for anything if he chose not to, it was a fully-equipped studio with a bathroom, kitchenette, walk-in closet, all-in-one dining room, living room and bedroom. Donald and Phillip sectioned off part of the large room to create a bedroom. The door that entered into the house, Phillip kept opened for Kayla and her baby brother, Kyle. They, often, came to see Phillip, and he cherished every time they ran into his room, "Cousin Phillip, Cousin Phillip, let's play," Kayla would say and Kyle would just say "pay, pay" and run to Phillip.

"What's Eritrea like?" asked Donna. "Grandma was the rock; she watched her family torn apart due to war. She birth ten children and all had to leave home at young ages to fight in the war or fled in hopes of life better somewhere else in the world. My father went back home and left my siblings and me with Grandma; he wanted us to live in a stable home because he fought with the Eritrean liberation forces. Eritrea has suffered for decades. Outside forces have always influenced the political climate; the U.S.-sponsored federation between Ethiopia and Eritrea triggered a 30-year war when Ethiopia annexed the strategic Red Sea territory. The Eritrean liberation forces fought with little outside help and defeated successive U.S. - and Soviet-backed Ethiopian regimes to win independence in 1993. The country abandoned after the cold war; Eritrea was born in ruins, with almost 85% of the population surviving on donated relief. The country was promised support for our self-reliance, but the U.S. still resists Eritrea's efforts to define our own policies. The U.S. and its European allies were critical of a reform that nationalizes urban and rural land, but guaranteed use rights to Eritreans, rather than privatizing it outright. Eritrea's effort to obtain development capital and foreign investment proved hard to attract, despite the almost complete absence of corruption or crime in the country, Phillip said.

"Grandma helped me in the village hospital; everything I learned in school, I taught her. The hospital would not have survived without her. She died there. She is the reason I am here in America; her last words were "Go my son, there is a world out there waiting for you." You would have loved her. I think of her every day. The hospital was low on supplies when she got sick, I think I could have done something to save her life, and I have regrets," Phillip said sadly.

There was a commotion at the dining room table. "Grandma," cried Kayla. Veronica grabbed her chest and gasped for air. "Mom, Mom," cried Donna as she jumped up, and ran to her. Baby Kyle started crying. Donald jumped up and ran to her. Phillip froze, time felt like it repeated itself; his newly adopted Grandmother is in distress.

Sherwood and Stephanie

"I have to go in, extra early, in the morning. We need to set up the command posts; the crowd expectation for the debate will probably double that of the press conference. This campaign has garnered much media attention; the security has to double for all events and we have to be ready," said Sherwood as he undressed for bed.

"Working on this campaign with Lolena has been an eye opener," said Stephanie "What do you mean?" he asked. "Well, politics, since President Obama was elected, I've gotten more involved, the most I have ever been, but working on this campaign, I think I got bitten by the political bug. No, I don't like the dirty politics. Silverstone Bay has been corrupted by dirty politics. It's going to take some time to clean up this city. I want to be an active part of the solutions; when Lolena is elected, I'm going to commission for a position on her cabinet," she said as she slid next to her husband and rubbed his bare chest.

"Baby, this conversation is getting me excited. Are the kids sleeping? I'm about to love you like we haven't done for a while," he said seductively. He kissed his wife passionately, she reciprocated the passion, and he pulled back and looked at her. Stephanie was a beautiful woman; kept her figure after four children. She played sports in high school and college and was very active with her children's sports activities. Sherwood loved every inch of her five-foot, six-inch, milk chocolate colored body. "I love you, sweetheart. Life would not be worth living if you weren't here with me," he said and moved on top of her and softly penetrated her. "I love you, being with you all these years has been my dream come true, Ummm, show me how much you love me," she said breathlessly. He move in and out, slow then faster, then slow, then faster. "Oh baby, you make me so hard, I can't seem to get enough of you," he said and continued to stroke her. "I'm coming baby, I'm coming...Um Um...here it comes...do you want me to take it out?" he managed to ask. "I feel you coming...you feel so good...no, don't take it out...I want it," she said as her eyes rolled back in her head. "Here it is for you, take it, take it, oh my god. I love you baby, I love you," he said and came with the power of a canon.

Nathaniel and Andrea

"It's good to see the boys so actively involved with the campaign. They all had a good time at the fundraiser," said Andrea. She and Nathaniel raised five foster boys one still lived with them. They decided if they were not able to have children on their own, they still had all that love to give; becoming foster parents was the answer. Nathaniel's love for horses gave the family years of enjoyment. So far, each child had performed in a rodeo over the years. The oldest child looks as if he will be the one to fall in his father's footsteps.

"Well with all the things that have been going on in Silverstone Bay, with their coach murdered and their friends murdered, they, like many residents, have had enough," he said, "I had to tell Nicholes (their oldest) he couldn't work on the security team until he got professional training. I think he might be joining the Silverstone Bay police department. He'd join tomorrow if I could convince Hercules to let him start."

"Can I get you anything to eat before I put the food away, baby?" asked Andrea. She was straightening up the kitchen, and Nathaniel stared at his wife as she tidied up her country-styled kitchen. She loved being in there, it was designed to accommodate her particular needs for her to create exquisite meals; her walk-in pantry stocked with every item that would allow her to cook a dish from any country in the world if she wanted and Nathaniel enjoyed every meal she prepared for the family. "When was the last time I told you I loved you?" he asked. "I don't remember. When was the last time you told me, do you remember?" she asked and batted her long eye lashes at him. He loved her eyes, her wide hips, her voluptuous breast, her thick thighs. "I'm sure it was just the other day, but right now I want to show you how much I love you," he said and grabbed her around her waist while she stood in front of the sink. He kissed the back of her neck. "That tickles," she said. He groped her breast and played with them. She braced herself against the sink. "Stand right there, I want to show you how much I love you just a little. Let me do all the work, just stand there," he said. He began to pull her pants down, he pulled her top over her head, unstrapped her bra. He felt her up and down. He moved his hand down to her clit and massaged her spot and she came. Before she regained her composure, he quickly unbuckled his pants, pulled out his hard manhood, and he entered her from behind. "You alright, baby? You feel so good. You're so wet," he moaned and stroked his wife for has long as he could; he felt the sensation coming and pounded her hard. "Here it comes, baby," he exploded inside of her.

Rafeki and Kena

"Do you want to make this official?" Rafeki asked his girlfriend. "Excuse me, are you talking to me?" asked Kena. "You're the only other person in this room, in this bed," he said as he made a circle around her belly button. The couple lay on top of their bed, listening to Bob Marley, burning incense and scented candles, sharing a bottle of wine and medical marijuana. "Okay, what makes it so important now? You haven't shown any interest before. Remember the time two years ago, I even asked you, and you said it wasn't the right time," Kena said, "than, a year ago, the marriage subject came up and nothing, soooo tonight you want to make this beautiful relationship official?" She says teasingly.

"Before you answer, let me do something for you," he said. "What do you want to do?" she asked. "No questions. Just lay there," he said. "Ok," she answered. He moved and balanced himself on top of her, kissed her softly on her lips and each area of her pretty face. He applied pressure against her body and grind against her pelvic. "Before I make love to you, can I taste you?" he whispered in her ear. Before she said anything, he moved down her body kissing, licking and sucking her proportionally shaped petite body. He kissed her navel then moved to her clit and licked, sucked and stroked his tongue all around her hot spot. He serviced her until she bucked and bucked and begged him to stop. "Oh my! Oh my! I'm coming. I'm coming," she screamed out, "Ahhhhhhhhhh! Ok, Ok, Ok."

Smokey Mike and Zelma

"It's getting late, baby, we need to get some rest," scolded Zelma. "Yeah, I know, but you know me, things have to be in order here at Dominic's. We've been so busy with the campaign, this place needed some attention before the big celebration after Lolena is elected mayor," Smokey addressed to his wife. "The race has been very interesting. It may have only been a few weeks of campaigning but doesn't it feel like the two years it takes to run for president?" She said exaggeratedly, "I don't think it was necessary for the opponent to play dirty politics. Well, it will make the debate very interesting. Lena didn't tell us exactly what she will be saying, she didn't want to have a mock rehearsal as she did when she made her announcement, but I can tell it will be interesting. I am proud of her; she is putting herself out there for the people of Silverstone Bay. I know she will do an excellent job," complimented Zelma; the charismatic character married to Smokey. It would take a person with lots of character to be able to stay married to Big Smokey Mike. He loves his dark-chocolate, gapped-tooth; short-fro wearing, curve-vá-shish, five-foot, three-inch tall, sarcastic-speaking, all-in-one friend and lover.

"Baby, thank you; I feel a need to thank you; you have stayed with me in spite of me and you still love me. Thank You," Smokey admitted. "Can you do me the favor of allowing me to show you my love for you?" he asked. She looked at her husband and ran through the inventory of her mind of the arsenal of information about this man on why she should question his love. "Show me," she said.

He walked over to her where she stood behind the bar, turned her around; placed a kiss on her luscious lips; unbuttoned her shirt; unzipped her pants and pull them down; sucked her plump breast; licked her clit; unbuckled his pants stroked his hard Johnson and inserted it into his wife with the thrust of a train and passion of a Latin lover. She spread her legs, wrapped her arms around her huge, manly man and let him have his way with her. "Come on baby, show me whatcha got," she said as she watched her husband stroke her hard. "Thank you, baby, thank you. This pussy is good. Give me more," he continued to stroke. "I love you and have to come now" he shouted and came into the woman who makes his life worth living.

Sonnie and Stacy

"Are you okay, honey? You seem awful quiet. Are you tired? You should be. We have been burning the candle at both ends during this short campaign season. I'm not complaining by any means, but I never been a part of a campaign ever. Well, I did some work on both Obama campaigns, but that didn't come close to the active role we have taken for the Win With Wynn campaign. That's such a catchy slogan. The Lolena Wynn Write Her In was pretty original, also. It was a good idea to use all the colors of the Crayola crayon box for the colors of the T-shirts. When you look at the symbolic nature of including all colors, well, the campaign is a

139

representation of including everyone here in Silverstone Bay. Wow, the pictures from the upcoming debate will be so colorful. If the number of people who showed up for the press conference show up for the debate, that will be pure beauty. There are going to be thousands of people at the debate, I know it. Every event we have held has been so packed. The security has been tight. There haven't been any incidences; Thank God." Stacy talked continuously. She was known to talk and talk and talk. She has a bubbly personality; that came in handy when she was the captain of her college and professional cheerleading squads. She met Sonnie when he played pro ball. Soon after, they hooked up; she hung up her pompoms. She was and is extremely limber. She put moves on her husband that ruined any chance of any woman to turn his head away from her.

"Tiffany told me she's in love with you," Sonnie said as he got in bed. Stacy continued organizing her outfit for tomorrow; brushed her teeth; washed her face; made sure all the electronics were plugged in and charging; did her floor exercises and said her prayers. She got in bed, looked at her husband, pulled the covers off him, looked at his naked body and kissed him. She straddled him, massaged his Johnson until he almost came, stopped and slid it inside of her and moved up and down as if she was riding on one of those mechanical bulls and rode her husband until he exploded inside of her. "I know, she told me," she said.

Code Red

"Good Morning, Beautiful," Hercules said to Lolena. "How did you sleep? Lolena turned over in bed and looked at him; he was dressed already; she loved the way he smelled. "Are you ready to get up? I prepared breakfast for you. Are you ready for this evening? We can rehearse again if you'd like. Do you need anything?" "Wait a minute, stop with all the questions for a few minutes," she interrupted. "How long have you been up? You're dressed?" she said with a tone of disappointment. "Excuse me, babe, I must be a little excited," he said.

Hercules was not excited; he was concerned. He was up early analyzing the letter delivered to his office:

Don't think it's over. This is not over. There is the matter of $5.5 million deposited in the Silverstone Bay Bank. If we don't get that money, Code Red is in full effect. Many lives are affected if the money is not delivered by 8:00 Election Day. On that day, we also expect the candidate Margaret Toolly elected. Lolena Wynn in no way will be the mayor. Have Phillip bring the money. He has access to the account. If we see this does not happen, we will not be afraid to use deadly force to make sure it does. Please take this letter seriously.

"I must get to my office early before the debate this evening. I should only be there a couple of hours. I'll get back here and take you to the campaign office." "I need to go by my office. I haven't been there these past few weeks. My assistant has done an excellent job of holding down the camp in my absence, but some things require my attention," she said. "Before you go, you can do something for me," she said and pulled the covers off to expose her naked body. Hercules was in a dilemma, make love to the woman he loves or tell her the reason he had to go was that her life depended on it. She looked mouthwatering. He wanted her bad, he needed her bad; he was about to burst just looking at her naked body. He wanted to be inside of her, if only for a few minutes. *"Maybe I could put it in for a few minutes, just to feel her wetness,"* he thought. "I love you, Lolena. I realize I love you more than life itself. If I don't leave at this moment, you might not be able to make it to the debate. I have something to put on you that when we're done, nobody will be able to move. So baby, I will be back to get you. Be ready," he said and quickly kissed her on the lips but took a moment to suck her breast and fondled her hot spot. He stopped, licked his finger, "I will finish you later," and left her panting.

****

The Band of Brothas convened in the back room of Dominic's. "I really hoped no bullshit would surface. We have to move fast. The fellas should be here later today. We still have access to the security team from San Francisco. Do we know when, where, what and how the note was delivered?" said Smokey. "The note was delivered to my office yesterday, but it was hand delivered by a messenger service," said Hercules, "We have to be on high alert from this point forward. We don't know exactly whom we are dealing with, but I will bet my life that it's the odd couple in the video." "They must be crazy. This one note includes extortion, murder, voter manipulation, and just plain stupidity," said Sherwood. "So by 8:00 tomorrow, they want $5.5 million delivered to them and hand the election over to Margaret, corrupt Mayor Burton's assistant. They think the people of Silverstone Bay will vote in 'more of the same'; they're crazy," said Smokey. "Yes, because they are that crazy, we can't put anything past them," said Rafeki. "This evening is the debate; that's not enough time to position a full fledge security opt. The condensed version is to join to the hips of your mates. They are targets. Call Phillip, he is a target. In reality, all citizens of Silverstone Bay are targets. If we hadn't stopped those shipments of fire power the night of the Mr. Michaels' Homecoming Game Celebration, I shudder to think the magnitude of what would have happened," said Sherwood.

"My Brothas are you Ready?" commanded Sonnie. "Ready for What?" they responded. "I said My Brothas are you Ready?" commanded Sonnie. "Yes, We Are!" and they walked into the light.

****

"Are you ready, sweetheart?" yelled Hercules when he walked into his house. There was no response. "Lolena, sweetheart, where are you?" There was no response. He glanced around his house to see if there was anything out of order. "Lolena!" He pulled out his revolver; looked around the kitchen, den, and office, went upstairs and saw the door to her bedroom closed; he called her again, "Lolena!" He pushed her door open; there she was sleep. He put his gun away and went over to her; shook her, she opened her eyes, removed the earphones, and glared at Hercules with fire in her eyes.

"Whoa, baby what's wrong? Did you hear me call you? What happened? What's going on? You know you are on a tight time schedule today, and I'm supposed to take you to your office right now. You're dress, but you don't look like you're ready to go." No response from her.

Lolena sat up, "I feel foolish." Hercules was confused, "Baby, talk to me." She got up, walked passed him and downstairs, out into the garage. He followed her. "I had my assistant bring my mail and

146

paperwork that I need to review. I felt it would save on time. As I was going through the boxes of correspondence, in between the letters, donations, bills I received this." She pulled out a manila envelope containing several photos of Hercules and an un-identified woman in bed in a multitude of sexual positions. There was a picture of a young man, approximate age 21 or 22, who bore a strong resemblance to Hercules. The letter read:

Dear Lolena, I'm writing you this letter as a seriously concerned citizen. You probably have looked at the pictures enclosed. I felt it was my civic duty to let you know with whom you are associating. Hercules McMarshall is not the person you think he is. He is heartless, abusive, a dead-beat dad, liar, cheater, manipulator, and untrustworthy. We met many years ago. He wanted to marry me. We had a baby out of wedlock. You see the resemblance. I moved to the area a few months ago, he found out where I lived, and he came over and forced himself upon me. I was afraid to go to the police because he is the police. When I saw that you are running for mayor, you are so beautiful, and I saw him standing next to you, I knew I had to speak out. You should know that man is an evil man. I will pray for you. Signed Concerned Citizen.

"I will admit it shocked me. I wasn't expecting it. Then, I had to determine if this is true or not true. Is this true, Hercules? I realize I love you, but I don't

147

really know you. You had a life before we met a few months ago. When I think about it, you haven't told me much about your life. I can see and feel that you are a good man, but I could be wrong. What is this Hercules? Can you explain this to me? Is this woman real? What is this? Tell me or am I just suppose to brush this off as junk mail? What was I thinking?" she blew a long breath out, shook her head, and dropped the pictures on the ground.

Hercules saw the photos containing pictures of him in extremely compromising position with the woman who had taken hundreds of pictures of him at the press conference. The woman whom he rejected years ago used those pictures to create this magnitude of incriminating pictures to send to the woman he loved and wanted no one to hurt her in any shape or form. "What a piece of work," he said. "Excuse me," Lolena snapped. "No baby, I'm not talking to you. The woman in the pictures is the piece of work," Hercules threw the pictures down. "Come over here, sit down," he said. She sat on the bench next to him. "The pictures are bullshit. What you need to do right now is dump that bullshit out of your head. I hate to tell you, there will probably be more bullshit coming.

148

I don't mean to talk so bluntly, but those are the facts. I know you know that. You are a strong woman. This woman is trying to shake you up because she's a sick bitch. I don't like to speak like that about a woman, but anybody who attempts to hurt you, doesn't have a snowball's chance in hell to survive the wrath of Hercules when it comes to hurting you in any fashion. Now, are you ready for the debate?" He said as he hugged her. "What about the young man in the pictures? Is he your son?" she asked. Hercules went and picked up the pictures, looked at it for a moment and said, "Yes."

The Debate?

The black stretch limo pulled up in front of City Hall; the plaza politically decorated for the occasion; packed with everybody; the media, supporters, security, tourists, vendors; you name them, were all there. The driver ran around to open the door for Lolena Wynn. The Lolena Wynn campaign organized the one and only debate for the candidates running for the mayor position. Since Mayor Burton was behind bars, the residents of Silverstone Bay self-nominated Lolena Wynn as the write-in candidate for which to vote. Margaret Toolly, City Manager of Silverstone Bay, self-nominated herself for the position. Based on her campaign strategy, she came out the starting block slinging mud directly at

Lolena Wynn. She accused her of lacking experience, her residency in Silverstone Bay, her college transcripts, her son's gang affiliations and her morals. She purchased thousands of dollars on airtime, print media and social media advertisement to promote the allegations repeatedly. During a television interview, she informed the viewing audience that she was moving up in the polls. During the same interview, the Wynn campaign called in to inform the listening audience that Lolena Wynn will be in front of City Hall at five o'clock sharp the evening before Election Day; if anyone wanted to debate her, be there.

At five o'clock on the dot, Lolena Wynn stepped out of the stretch limo. The Band of Brothas, dressed in standard black attire: tight, muscle-showing silk T-shirts, slacks, boots, shades, and berets stood in a two-line formation and walked Lolena Wynn to one of the podiums set up in front of City Hall. The crowd cheered for several minutes. The band played the Win With Wynn theme song; streamers were shot up in the air, balloons hung from every tree, lamp posts, pole, bench, anything strong enough to wrap string around it held a balloon. The music and the cheering continued until Stephanie went to the podium set in the middle of the three podiums. She tapped the mike and heard the amplified noise over the crowd. "Hello Silverstone Bay!" she announced. The crowd roared for another five minutes. "ARE YOU READY FOR A DEBATE?!" "Whoa Who! Yeah! Bring it On! Lolena, Lolena, Lolena!" cheered from the crowd. "Well, Alright," she said. "It looks like it's time to get this party started. You all sounds like you're ready to go. Ok, before we get starts, let's go over some rules. Wait a minute, before we get to the rules; let's make sure everyone who wants to participate is in position. Ok, I see Ms. Wynn is here. Is there anyone else who wants to participate?" she said as she noticed there was no one at the empty podium. The crowd quietly murmured wondering where was the opponent. The door to city hall opened, and Margaret Toolly walked out and positioned herself in front of the empty podium. The crowd politely clapped. "So it looks like there's going to be a debate," announced Stephanie. "Now, let's get started. Here are the rules, Please be courteous, considerate and conscientious. This is a unique situation, one Silverstone Bay has never experienced. The two women who stand before you are write-in candidates, the campaign season was extremely short so for those of you who have not made up your mind, (there was some sarcastic chuckling coming from the crowd) now is an opportunity for you to get to know the candidates better. The forum will be flexible, I will ask questions, each candidate can ask the other questions, and we will take a couple of questions from the audience. The last thing I will mention is for those who have not voted yet, the polls open at seven o'clock in the morning," she informed the audience.

"To see who goes first, I will toss a coin," Stephanie said. Lolena spoke, "Excuse me, Stephanie, there is no need for that, Ms. Toolly may go first, Proceed Ms. City Manager," Lolena said in a President Obama debate move. She was greeted with Rooney snare from her opponent. "Well, thank you," Margaret said, "Good Evening, for those of you who don't know me, my name is Margaret Toolly. I am the City Manager of Silverstone Bay. I stand for righteousness, high standards, intelligence, honesty, and I don't associate with known gang members."

"Oh, no she didn't say that" "She's taking it to that level" "Whooo!" "Boo!" were comments that came from the crowd. "Calm down, people," said Stephanie as she rolled her eyes at Margaret and turned to Lolena and said, "You got this." Lolena gave her the sista look as to say, "It's on now."

Lolena turned to the crowd, "Good Evening, I'm Lolena Wynn, and I am your write-in candidate for Mayor of Silverstone Bay." The crowd went wild. "Thank you, thank you. Your support means so much to me. However, it's not about me; it's about you the residents of Silverstone Bay. I am confident that with your vote for me, remember the campaign slogan: Lolena Wynn Write Her In, we can rebuild Silverstone Bay. We can right some of the wrongs that were committed by the leadership that participated in the deterioration and destruction of a city that has been the home of your families for generations. Speaking of homes, my opponent has implied I am not a resident of Silverstone Bay. The crowd laughed. To put at ease anyone who may question my residency, I made available online at www.WinWithWynn.com copies of my utility bills, subscriptions, voter registration card, and bank statements dated back three years ago which clearly indicates my Silverstone Bay address; clear evidence of my residency here in Silverstone Bay.

"My opponent has questioned my education; well I'm not even going to dignify that with a response; I don't feel a need to stoop to that level. However, I have some people with whom I graduated from college, summa cum laude, here to show their stepping talents for you all. Ladies and gentlemen, here to step for you, the distinguished women of Delta Sigma Theta, Eta Omega chapter of SJSU." The ladies came out of nowhere, all of a sudden, there they stood, in line formation, wearing the sorority colors, red and white, red boots, white pants, red tank top. Lolena left the podium and stood in formation with her sistas. The crowd went ballistic. Margaret looked annoyed. The step leader began, and the sistas stepped:

I said my sistas
One step two step stop
I said my sistas
One step two step stomp, stomp
Delta Call
Clap Clap Clap; Clap Clap
Stomp kick, stomp kick, stop
Shimmy shake left, shimmy shake right
Turn to the left, turn to the right
One step two step stop
One step two step stomp, stomp
Whip hip around left, Whip hip around right
Pose

Lolena stepped out of formation, went back to the podium, and spoke without even breathing hard, "Whew, well how did you like that! Thank you my

155

sistas. Wow, I haven't stepped like that for years." The crowd continued to cheer; you could hear shout outs from other sororities and fraternities in the crowd. "We love you, Lolena," shouted from the crowd. "I love you back," responded Lolena.

"We saw and heard the bombardment of ads, from my opponent, accusing my son of associating with known gang members; from what I saw, you would have thought I was raising the next John Gottie. Now, again, I will not dignify any of that nonsense with a response. First, you don't have the right to attempt to slander the character of my son and second, it's your boss sitting behind bars, as we speak, for his criminal behavior and gang association?" Lolena said and pivoted in Margaret's direction daring her to utter a word in her own defense. Margaret continued to stand there in angry silence. "However, I would like to take this opportunity to introduce my son. Alvin, would you please come up here." Alvin made his way to the podium, kissed his mother on the cheek and gave her a hug. "I would like to introduce the sunshine in my eyes, my son, Alvin Wynn. He is an up and coming producer and he and his group, J-Knock Ent., want to perform for you today and I told him to keep it clean." "Thank you mom, I love you, and I am proud of you. You will be a rockin' Mayor," said Alvin as he took the mike and transformed to his alter ego: Sixty B Mackin.

J-Knock Ent. came to the front of the City Hall, the beat produced by Sixty roared through the speakers, the crowd fell into time with the groove. "Y'all feel alright! I'm Alvin aka Sixty B Mackin and we are J-Knock Ent. and we're gangsters alright, gangsters for love, gangsters for peace, gangsters for what is right. So if it's okay with you, we would like to rap to you." The crowd was into an uproar again.

Lolena Wynn Write Her In
When you wake up in the morning
And move your feet
Move to the polls and hear the beat
Silverstone Bay will see the day
When Lolena B Wynn will rule the day
So when you wake up in the morning
And move your feet
Step to the polls and hear the beat
Lolena Wynn Write Her In!

The ovation for J-Knock Ent. went on until Lolena spoke, "Baby, thank you. You all hit it out of the ballpark with that performance. If that is your gang affiliation, gangsta for love, I am sure you will get more members.

"My opponent's attacks require no explanations from me, but I want to say to you, residents of Silverstone Bay, when she attempted to question my morals and experience, she made a serious mistake because my morals and my experience are my strength. You see, some people get in bed with the devil in order to step on someone else's character. What Ms. Margaret Toolly did was to use a heinous crime committed against me and twisted it to paint a picture that I was found in a drunken stooper after a night of wild partying; there isn't anything further from the truth. I'm going to tell you all the truth. I'm going to tell you what happened to me over twenty years ago when I was a soldier in the military. Until this day, I have spoken of that incident only one other time in my life. I buried it so deep inside me that I almost forgot it happened. I made the choice not to let it define my life. Fellow soldiers viciously raped me; they drugged me at the nightclub; drove me to the motor pool and repeatedly raped me. The military gave me an honorable discharge and mandated my silence. I stand before you, today, not as a victim of rape but a woman with the strength of a lion, elephant and tiger, all in one. Therefore, I say to my opponents, **Really, Do you want to Mess with Me**."

The crowd went ballistic again.

"In conclusion, tomorrow is Election Day, we all have the choice to move Silverstone Bay in a new direction. It's going to take some time, but it won't take as much time if you vote the person into office that is on your side. I am on your side. I witnessed, we all witnessed, the actions of people, in office, who did not have the best interest of the residents of Silverstone Bay in mind. So tomorrow you know what to do, and if you happen to forget, just remember how J-Knock Ent. so eloquently said it in a rap song:

Lolena Wynn Write Her In
When you wake up in the morning
And move your feet
Move to the polls and hear the beat
Silverstone Bay will see the day
When Lolena B Wynn will rule the day
So when you wake up in the morning
And move your feet
Step to the polls and hear the beat
Lolena Wynn Write Her In!

Election Day

"Good Morning, Beautiful," Hercules said. Lolena looked at him. She looked at his eyes and noticed the sex appeal oozing out of them as he spoke. His nose sat on his face not to be too obvious but yet apparent as you looked at him. His smile seemed to come easily now. There was more opportunity to notice his gold-trimmed front tooth against his perfect set of pearly whites. His clean-shaven face and baldhead allowed his dark chocolate skin to glow as the morning sunlight beamed in through the windows. *"Today is Election Day, I made it; soon my life will change more drastic then it has already. Soon he will make love to me and not think about the campaign. Yes, the campaign is officially over today," she thought.*

"Hello, sweetheart, have you heard anything I just said? I see you looking at me and you seem to be nodding your head as if you hear me, but I don't hear anything coming out of that pretty mouth of yours," he said. Lolena snapped out of her trance. "Okay, I'm here and present. It's just that each time you come to the door and stand there all suited up and smelling so good, it just sends me into another world," she said.

Hercules walked over to the bed, pulled the covers back, drank in her naked body, took her hand, put it on his now erected joystick, and said, "Feel that, it's yours tonight. I want you to do anything and everything to it, just like I am going to do everything to…" and he moved his hand down to her hotspot and played with it, he slid his finger in and out all while keeping her hand held up against him but stopped. "Damn, I'm about to burst, Baby, but I have to get you through this day safe and sound. I have to stay focus. You have to stay focus." He pulled her out of bed, wrapped his arms around her and said, "You are all I need to breathe another breath."

****

161

The bright sun woke Silverstone Bay up on Election Day. The birds chirped. A gentle breeze cleaned the air. Tropical music filled to the air at all public places. The decorations from the debate the evening before still landscaped the plaza. The sidewalks and streets swept clean of debris and litter. The storghes, shops, restaurants, cafes, service stations, churches, schools and city hall opened earlier than usual. Several of those facilities were voting polls. At seven o'clock in the morning, the people started lining up to cast their ballot.

"This is Chisti Barber coming to you live in front of city hall. If you weren't with us last night, we are at the location where the mayoral debate was held. The debate proved to be more than just a mundane political debate. It was much more than that. The two opponents attended, but we can't report much activity from the Margaret Toolly camp. After she introduced herself and stated her platform, that pretty much all she said, she spoke at total forty-five words during the entire three-hour debate. On the other side, however, Lolena Wynn treated the thousands of attendees to an evening of entertainment from her sorority sisters and the candidate participated in the step show. Her son for whom her opponent accuses of having gang connection performed. As the debate ended, Lolena with dignity and grace shared with the audience the horrific experience of rape she endured while she was in the military. The debate proved to be an event that Silverstone Bay won't be forgetting for many years to come."

"If you look in back of me, you can see the lines forming at the voting polls. Based on what we see now, it looks as if Silverstone Bay might experience the largest voter turnout in the city's history. Let's see if we can get someone to speak to us on camera about this election. Excuse me sir, I'm Chisti Barber from Channel Five News. I see you are out early to cast your ballot. What has this election meant to you?" The reporter held the mike to the senior man looked to be in his later sixties wearing a dark blue warm-up outfit. "Good Morning, Chisti, I watch you on television and now I'm here talking to you, go figure. Well, all I'm going to say is I hope the best candidate wins. In all my years voting here in Silverstone Bay, I am glad my choice of candidates to write in is Lolena Wynn." "There you have it from what obviously a happy Lolena Wynn supporter. Stay with us throughout the day as we bring you Election Day activities," Chisti signs off.

****

"Code Red is going according to plan," Jennifer smirked as she watched Chisti Barber on television; "Margaret is proving to be smarter than I thought. She held her tongue at the debate, very wise of her. The letter deliveries went according to plan, the heavy guns arrived and moving into place as we speak. Yes, Code Red is working," she said fiendishly.

"I have a guaranteed plan in place if for some reason something goes wrong," said Mr. G. "There will be no fuck ups this time." "Really, what is that?" she asked. "It's better to keep that close to my chest," he said with icicles falling off each word. She sat up in bed and glared at him. "Well we are keeping secrets from each other now. Is it a secret where you went last night? You left me in this room alone for a long time," she inquired.

Mr. G got out of bed, went to the bathroom for a while, came back and got back in bed. He sat up, spread his legs open, and pulled her between them turning her to face him. With his firm hands clenching her biceps, he pulled her close and glared into her eyes; he saw the emptiness that ran deep into her soul. He lowered her down and pushed her head down between his legs. His cock was hard and stood up at attention. "You know what to do with it," he moaned. She instinctively opened her mouth and began sucking him. She sucked and licked him with pleasure. She liked his cock. "Oooo, this is good, just the way I like it," she said between lavishes. He laid back and enjoyed. His head went back; he rested his arms on the bed and fantasized about getting head while he was getting head. She worked hard on his dick; she would stop to jerk him off and then go back and suck him more. She was getting excited, she played with her titties, and he played with her titties. "Stop, get over here and lay on your back," he instructed. He spread her legs, slid his dick inside her, and fucked her. "Um, take that. Um take that. Yes, you bitch, take that," he groaned, and then he pulled out and unloaded on her belly. "There's more in there, come finish me off," he instructed again. She sat up on her knees and finished him off; he unloaded the last of his come in her mouth. He got out of bed, turned around, and said to her, "Don't ask me where I've been. Are we clear on that?"

****

165

The protocol for handling the ballots added extra challenges this election; extra workers volunteered to count the thousands of ballots that required manual handling since the majority of the ballots would indicate the write-in candidate of the voter's choice. A designated crew picked up the ballots boxes and delivered them to an undisclosed destination. The crew assigned to count the ballot first reviewed the ballot to determine who earned that ballot, they input the data into the secure database, the ballot is marked counted, put in another box and the box of marked ballot makes its way to the final storage destination under heavy security via the final ballot crew.

Jessica, the voter ballot supervisor, opened the back door to accept the boxes of ballots delivered at ten o'clock in the morning. The crew begins the counting and inputting. At noon, Jessica accepts the next delivery of ballots. The data center is bustling. At two o'clock, Jessica accepts the third delivery of ballots. The data center continues nonstop inputting data. Jessica accepts the catered lunches delivered to the makeshift lunchroom at noon. At three o'clock, there is a shift change and Jessica accepts the next delivery of ballots. The data center works in over drive mode. At four o'clock, Jessica accepts the next delivery of ballots. She starts to feel warm and then breaks out into a sweat. "Hey Jessica, I'm sent over to relief you. Looks like I'm just in time, you don't look too good," said Helen. "I don't feel too good right now. All of a sudden, something hit me," and then things went black for Jessica.

****

Alvin is feeling anxious. He enjoyed staying in the penthouse of the Silverstone Bay Executive Suite Inn, but now it's time for him to go home to his own house and sleep in his own bed. "Hey babe, you packed?" he asked his girlfriend. Sheila, who was still packing said, "Just about. Are you ready? Why are you pacing the floor? Before I forget to tell you, this has been an adventurous past few weeks. It's actually been the most exciting thing that has ever happened to me. I had to act as a decoy, we sang a love song for your mother, I met some famous people, and this place is so enchanting. Thank you, Alvin. Oh, if it doesn't bother you too much, can I tell you I love you?" Alvin stopped pacing for a moment and contemplated the statement. "Relax, I'm not proposing marriage or anything like that. I'm just saying, I think you are a really nice person. You have been a perfect gentleman these past few weeks, you're smart, funny, cute, and we make beautiful music together. You know if we make beautiful music together, we probably will make beautiful babies together," she said teasingly. He looked at her with such an expression of fear on his face. "Relax, I said, I'm just kidding. Calm down. Breathe," she said.

Alvin resumed pacing the floor. "Hey Alvin, really, I was just kidding around," she said as she looked at him go back and forth. "Girl, I know you're kidding, I just got things heavy on my mind. I mean today is Election Day and tonight they are going to announce the winner of the mayor's race. My mother is going to be the mayor, I don't doubt that, but I have this sinking feeling that something is going to go wrong," and then he bent his head down, and Sheila saw a tear drop from his eye.

****

"This is Chisti Barber reporting to you live from City Hall on the Election Day evening here in Silverstone Bay. The city has not been this excited about an election, well, ever. Reports are coming in that the lines were long, but there have been no reported incidents. All in all, the day was filled with excitement and anticipation. No reports from the ballot counting center except that a supervisor fainted; probably from exhaustion. I'm sure you can imagine they are working overtime to get all the ballots counted. Stay tuned with us as we bring to you up to the minute details on the famous mayor election in Silverstone Bay. This evening at nine o'clock, both candidates will be in front of city hall to hear the results. As you can see, people have already started gathering. Wait a minute; I'm getting some news about preliminary results…what was that… has that information been verified? Okay. Excuse me, ladies and gentlemen, for that interruption. We will be back shortly. Please stay tuned," Chisti quickly signs off the air.

The Results

The Lolena Wynn Campaign crew gathered one last time at RapCity. Peace B Out stood in front of the group and said, "It has been my extreme honor and pleasure to have had this place, my place, as campaign headquarters. I have gotten to know all of you and I consider you my family, I hope you consider me part of your family," as he choked up a little. Lolena walked over to him and gave him a hug. She wiped a tear from her eye. "Wow, what an emotional day. I don't know about you, but this feels unbelievable. We have come so far in such a short amount of time. Since we can pull off a phenomenal campaign like this, imagine what we will do when we become mayor; yes I said we. Don't think this is over, this is just the beginning. We now have a city to run, and it's going to take a village to run it," she said.

Smokey Mike and Zelma stood up, "We agree, we did a great job, and we look forward to many years of progress, prosperity and possibilities."

Sonnie and Stacy stood up, "We are proud of you Lolena, we would not have been able to look so good if you weren't as dynamic as you are."

Nathaniel and Andrea, "I, for one, am glad today's Election Day. I'm not sure how many more times we could have rescued you from the enormous crowds you attracted everywhere you went. You know I can't bring Black Bucket everywhere you go." The group chuckled.

Rafeki and Kena stood up, "Brothas and Sistas, we did good. I'm proud of us."

Sherwood and Stephanie, "Y'all sure y'all want to do this, you know, the results aren't in yet, we still have time to get out." The group laughed.

Hercules stood up and went over to Lolena, "You are the strongest, bravest, prettiest woman I know. I can't go into life without you with me and me without you, would you do me the honor..." His phone rang, and he recognized the number, "Hello sir, thank you for calling. Yes, we are anxiously waiting for the results. Yes, she's standing right here. I'm sure she'll love to hear from you!" Hercules handed her his phone but put it on speaker first, "Hello, Lolena? Is this Lolena Wynn of the most famous mayor election ever! I like your slogans: Win With Wynn and Lolena Wynn Write Her In; their catchy; almost as catchy as mine." Lolena could recognize that voice anywhere. "Hello Lolena are you there?" "Yes, Sir, I mean Yes, Sir Mr. President!"

****

Lolena sat in the back of the limo alone, quietly contemplating her thoughts. The driver took the scenic route around the city that looked so beautiful at night. As the limo got closer to city hall, the sky illuminated from the lights decorating downtown; she knew her moment was here. "Here we are Ms. Wynn," the driver announced.

****

The Band of Brothas met to tighten the details. "Did you reach, Phillip?" asked Hercules. "Yes, I did," said Smokey. "Is everything in place?" asked Hercules. "Let's go over the details again.

Sherwood and Sonnie you're stationed over here to the left of the stage. Smokey and Rafeki over here in this area should give you a good vantage point. Nathaniel, you and I will be closest to the target." Hercules paused for a moment. "What's up Herk?" asked Sherwood. "You know, I'm feeling something. It's gnawing in my gut. I don't like the feeling. I remember the last time I had this feeling. Tonight, I wanted it to be extra special. I hoped to have proposed to her earlier this evening, but the President interrupted my proposal." "Ain't that about the worst thing that could ever happen to a person who is about to be elected mayor of a city is to receive a congratulations call from the President of the United States. Let me see, call from President or proposal from boyfriend," Sherwood says as he pretends to balance an invisible object between his two hands. "Let's see, the President wins out," they all laugh at the teasing of Hercules' self-made pity party. "Keep it up, man, you know I can get you back somehow. Remember, I could be your boss soon. Anyways, I don't need to tell any of you that the threat is real tonight, so everyone keep your eyes, ears and the eyes behind your head open. Are we ready?" he said. "Yes we are!" They say in unison.

173

The ballot counting data center was feverously working inputting ballot results as fast as they came in. The polls closed and the last drop off was delivered, signed in and processed. Helen set at the main computer and logged into the backdoor of the database. "Okay, let me tweak the results for this precinct, this one, this one and this one," she said, as she made sure to delete her tracks in the system. She placed a call and said, "It's done."

****

Margaret Toolly sat at her computer and logged into the site where she viewed the data, keyed in additional data, logged out making sure she covered her tracks and texted the message: It's done. She then took a moment to contemplate her next strategy. She poured herself a drink, leaned back in the chair and reminisced about the night before after she left the debate and Mr. G met her in the empty mayor's office. They laughed about how they were going to run Silverstone Bay after the election. "They really think they are going to win this election. Did you see those people cheering, laughing and dancing for that nigger woman? They won't be laughing tomorrow," Mr. G said. "No, they won't. They don't know the wheels have already started turning on the private prison complex to be constructed at the old military base. One of the first people there will be her nigger son and his so-called crew. They will be able to create all the rap songs they want to since they will be the one's charge for murder," she said with venom in her voice. "Did you get the cameras set up, I want to see everything tomorrow, up close and personal," he asked. "Yes, you will be able to see everything up close and personal," she acknowledged. She thought about him when he walked up behind her and groped her breast and grinded her ass with his pelvic. The dry fuck went on for a few minutes until he ripped her blouse off, turned her around and bit her nipples and neck leaving marks on her body. She had to camouflage them tonight with makeup and scarves. He pulled down her pants and panties and fingered her until she came. He stepped back, unbuckled and unzipped his pants. He gave her the condom, which she promptly preceded to place on his cock. "Before you put that on, get down to your knees and suck it first," he ordered. She did as instructed. She enjoyed doing that for Mr. G. She had hopes and dreams of satisfying him for a long time. "Stop, stand up and turn around and bend over," he instructed. She did as

175

instructed. He entered her from behind and pounded her into hysteria. He pulled out, yanked off the condom and jerked his come on her back. "Here, take the rest," he instructed and she did as instructed.

Margaret realized she was fondling herself when she snapped out of her fantasy when she heard cheering coming from outside.

****

Chisti Barber saw Hercules and quickly ran over to him. "Can I talk to you?" she asked. "Can it wait, the results are about to be announced," he said. "It's about the results," she said. He looked at her, then at the time, then he looked for Lolena, but he didn't see her.

****

Silverstone Bay was electrified. The plaza and the entire downtown area was packed with people. You would have thought it was New Year's Eve in Time Square. The security was tight. The media army covered every angle they could think of. Interviews were conducted everywhere people gathered. The weather was a pleasant seventy-eight degrees. Several business establishments stayed opened. Street vendors took advantage of the large crowd, and a person could find food, souvenirs, or

176

campaign paraphernalia on every corner. The anticipation continued to grow; the crowd started chanting all the Lolena Wynn campaign slogans or songs. People began to shout for her "Where's Lolena?"

****

Jennifer and Mr. G ordered plates of food and several bottles of alcohol. Two television monitors were set up in their suite. On one set, the local channel five station aired. On the other monitor, the view was from the camera set up by Margaret Toolly. The view was the stage area looking towards the crowd. In the corner of that monitor was the view from the camera Margaret wore on her lapel. "In five minutes, the announcement will be made," Jennifer said. "I will be so glad, now we can get away from this place. I have grown bored with it. The people, the city, the weather; I'm bored. Take me away from here," she said to him. He didn't turn to look at her, didn't say a word, didn't move. He sat there watching the monitors. "There he is, right there, you see him, Phillip, Mr. E's butler and it looks like he has the briefcase. That's right, have a seat right there," Mr. G said as if he could hear him through the monitors. "There she is, that never-to-be mayor of Silverstone

177

Bay, Lolena Wynn. She looks troubled; my letter must have really disturbed her. There is Mr. Hercules, and it looks like he is troubled too. Yes, they are all in place. There's her son. There are the body guards, but they won't be able to help you now," Jennifer squealed with excitement. "It's nine o'clock on the dot."

****

"Ladies and Gentleman, can I have your attention, please. It's nine o'clock, and we have the results of the Election," said the city official.

The crowd silenced. At that very moment, there were several bright lights, there were several swoosh, swoosh, swoosh sounds heard, and time stood still. Screams broke the silence; people ran in all directions, the entire plaza was in pandemonium.

"This is Chisti Barber, I am at the plaza where one moment, the election results were about to be announced and then the next moment we all had to run for our lives. I can't get any closer right now but up by the staging area where the candidates sat, there are several dead bodies.

Epilog

"This is Chisti Barber, live at the scene. This is a horrific event. People a screaming and crying. There was an explosion and gunfire. We are held back here. We can't get too close to the stage. I am sorry to report that there are several dead bodies. I can see from where I am standing people are lying on the ground. Excuse me…What was that? Please repeat that! No, I can't get any closer. Ok, I am just getting word that…"

"Where's Lolena Wynn? Where's Lolena?" could be heard from several people above the pandemonium.

"Mom! Mom! Mom! Where are you?"

"I saw Hercules down by the stage. Where is he? I can't find him."

"Let the authorities through! Let them through!"

"Have you seen my husband, he was down there next to the stage!"

"Mam, Mam Can you hear me? Can you hear me?"

"I can't seem to find a pulse."

"Take the wounded victims over there. They set the triage unit over there. Take the ones that did not make it over there behind city hall. The crime unit is stationed back there.

"Rope all this section off. This is an active crime scene," said Sherwood. "Keep all those people back. Move! I said move!"

"That went like clockwork, right down to the last minute," said Mr. G.

"Code Red is on fire tonight," squealed Jennifer. There was a knock at the door of their room. "Looks like she's on time."

38767030R00117

Made in the USA
Charleston, SC
17 February 2015